Praise for *Uplifting Service*

"Read this book, apply the steps. Watch your culture transform and your perspective on service change forever. Ron Kaufman has unlocked the mystery of service. Get ready for a magnificent journey into a new world."

Marshall Goldsmith
Bestselling Author of *What Got You Here Won't Get You There*

"Ron Kaufman has pinpointed a massive wound in society, and offers a strategy on how to uplift the world around us. For mankind, it's transformational. For business, it's a clean and clear path to a sustainable competitive advantage. This book is long overdue, and will certainly create a legendary shift."

Thomas Moran
Director, Customer and Partner Experience
Microsoft Operations

"*Uplifting Service* is a much needed breath of fresh air for our troubled times. Service authority Ron Kaufman has distilled his global perspective into a blueprint for delighting customers. This is a critical skill now that social media has amplified customers' voices many times over. If you have customers you must read this now."

Stephen M. R. Covey and Greg Link
Bestselling Authors of *Smart Trust*

"*Uplifting Service* gets to the bottom of what every great business should be, and then uplifts it. Ron's message is timely and the architecture he provides for building a service culture is timeless. This is a necessary book for every business."

Ann Rhoades
Board Member, JetBlue Airways
Bestselling Author of *Built on Values*

UPLIFTING
SERVICE

The Proven Path

to Delighting Your Customers, Colleagues,

and Everyone Else You Meet

RON
KAUFMAN

The following are registered trademarks or trademarks of Ron Kaufman Pte Ltd: Ron Kaufman®, Uplifting Service™, UP! Your Service®, the word "UP" in a balloon device®, the "Criminal to Unbelievable!" device®, the "Explore, Agree, Deliver, Assure" device®, The 12 Building Blocks of Service Culture™, The Six Levels of Service™, The Cycle of Service Improvement™, Up the Loyalty Ladder™, Bouncing Back with Service Recovery™, Clear, Kept Promises™, Closing the Loop™, Service Transactions and Perception Points™, The BIG Picture™, Uplifting Service Champions™.

All references to trademarked properties are used in accordance with the Fair Use Doctrine and are not meant to imply that this book is a product for advertising or other commercial purposes.

"UPLIFTING SERVICE: The Proven Path to Delighting Your Customers, Colleagues, and Everyone Else You Meet"

Published by Evolve Publishing, Inc.
www.evolvepublishing.com

10 9 8 7

ISBN 978-0-9847625-5-2 — paperback
        978-0-9847625-0-7 — hardcover
        978-0-9847625-9-0 — ebook

Table of Contents

SECTION FOUR: LEARN

SECTION FIVE: DRIVE

A Personal Path to Service

For the past 40 years I have been on a mission to improve the world. The vision that motivates and sustains me is a world in which everyone is educated and inspired to excel in service to others.

In support of this mission, I have flown more than ten million miles, visited three hundred cities, and worked with businesses in every industry from high fashion to high technology, government agencies, schools, associations, and voluntary service organizations. I help people become better service providers, and help organizations build uplifting and self-sustaining service cultures.

I define service as taking action to take care of someone else. Or, in commercial terms: *Service is taking action to create value for someone else.* The surprising upside is that improving the service you give someone else also benefits you. Providing uplifting service to others naturally enriches your relationships, improves your network of support, and contributes to your own success.

People often ask me where I get my intense passion for this topic of uplifting service. I consistently and candidly reply, "I get my passion from you." It delights me to see people succeed by contributing to the lives of others. That's what this book will do for you: show you how you can add more value to others, and gain more for yourself.

Life Lessons

Unusual people and events have powerfully shaped my life, and the lessons I've learned from them are the roots of my unrelenting passion. My grandmother was my earliest inspiration. She taught kindergarten in New York City for 40 years, and when I visited her class, I felt like the most important person in the world. My grandmother made everyone feel like the most important person in the world.

She'd give one child a compliment and give another a helping hand. She'd read to one group while answering questions from another. She'd separate two fighting five-year-olds and manage to make them both feel good. And at the end of the day, she reassured every parent that his or her messy, noisy, rambunctious child was the most precious miracle in her classroom.

What amazed me was my grandmother's ability to do this all day, all year, for 40 years. Every time she made a child smile, she seemed to get more energized, like her battery was being charged over and over again. She got as much juice out of teaching the kids as they got from being with her. The lesson I learned from watching my grandmother work was as clear to me then as it is today: *providing service to someone else gives you something back. Making other people feel good somehow makes you stronger.* Grandma Bea was the first great teacher in my life. Her intention to serve was the most memorable thing about her. She called it love.

While my grandmother taught me the beauty of service, a Frisbee disc opened the door to a life of serving others.

I am not a tall person. Actually, I'm short. Most team sports were out of my reach as a kid. All that changed when a local high school teacher, Al Jolley, introduced the Frisbee game called Ultimate in our school, and formed a team that anyone could join. But still, because I was short and not very good at throwing or catching a Frisbee, I was often the last person picked.

Dan Buckley was a much more experienced player, and he sported a heart as big as his Frisbee-flinging sidearm throw. He not only picked the smaller people so we could play; he actually threw the disc to us and encouraged us whether we caught it or dropped it, made a decent or another lousy throw. My grandmother had every reason to be nice to little people; she was a kindergarten teacher and she was my grandmother. Dan had no apparent external motivation for being so generous. His reason came from within.

The first official rule in Ultimate is called "the Spirit of the Game." It holds players fully accountable for their behavior on a playing field with no referees. Dan did not just follow this rule; he lived it and I learned a powerful lesson from his example. *Everybody wants to play in this life. Give people enough encouragement and opportunity, and they will rise to the occasion, often surprising you with their commitment and contribution.*

After high school I enrolled at Brown University where I studied history and was captain of the Ultimate team. On the Frisbee field we learned how to work and win together on a small scale. As a student of human history, I was shocked by how often people all over the world fail at living well together on a large scale. Humanity seems to have a long-standing addiction to misunderstanding, mistrust, and armed conflict. Hardly the spirit of the game I thought we could be playing.

In my studies, I wasn't as interested in learning why war broke out as I was curious to understand how people came back together. Trade and commerce play roles in reconnecting people after war. But I was more intrigued by the endearing and emotionally enduring connections: sporting events, pen pals, student exchanges, and sister cities. I wondered if I could make this kind of contribution to other people's lives, make a bit of difference, and maybe even make this world a better place to work, live, and love.

So I took my curiosity and Frisbees to Europe where I studied during fall and winter and travelled madly in spring and summer. I slept on trains, ate in vegetable markets, and engaged with the people I met in every direction. I taught Frisbee to families in parks and was invited into their homes for dinner. I played Frisbee on the beach and ended up at parties with new friends. I sold Frisbees in the streets and was overlooked by the police who simply smiled.

Whether on Scandinavia's modern trains, Rome's vibrant streets, or Morocco's earthy squares, I discovered that I could lift people's eyes and spirits with my simple piece of plastic. Riding with the wind by day and on rumbling trains at night, my life became a real-world expression of the Frisbee advertising slogan, "You just can't do it alone."

Even during those carefree days I was learning something useful—that effective methods for connecting people can also be easy to apply. *Uplifting someone else's spirit can be as simple as putting a smile on your face, a compliment in your voice, or a Frisbee on your finger.*

My flying discs were simple tools for creating connections, over-coming fears, evoking—and at times provoking—full participa-tion. Getting people involved gave me deep satisfaction. Getting people to play together gave me even more.

Dan "Stork" Roddick worked for the Frisbee manufacturing com-pany Wham-O. He heard about my adventures overseas and sent me business cards that read "Ron Kaufman, International Repre-sentative, International Frisbee Association." This was the equiva-lent of deputizing an evangelist to take on the world. So I did.

I created a company called Disc Covering the World and spent two more years crossing borders and organizing flying disc tourna-ments, festivals, clinics, and family play days everywhere I went. I rallied students to an international Ultimate game in London's Hyde Park and created an Official Frisbee Sanctuary with a willing youth hostel warden in Belgium. I served as Master of Ceremonies at the Smithsonian Frisbee Festival in Washington, D.C., the Mil-ton Keynes Bowl Air Day in the United Kingdom, and the World Frisbee Championships at the Rose Bowl in California.

Throughout these adventures, Stork was an encouraging patron, collaborator, advisor, and friend. He saw the world through the lens of a sociologist and believed that we could shape culture with festivals and sports, that we could popularize the Spirit of the Game. We shared the dedication of those who uplift themselves by deliberately serving others. But we didn't call it service at the time. We called it play.

One year when I was Master of Ceremonies at the Rose Bowl, I discovered that collective energy is malleable and people who or-ganize others bear a responsibility to shape that energy with care. One hot summer day, someone pushed a scrawled note onto my clipboard: "A big dog is barking desperately in a white van in the parking lot with all the windows rolled up. It's hot!!" I looked up at the enormous crowd and paused, then took a deep breath and announced, "Ladies and Gentlemen. If you drove here today in a white van with a big dog, your canine friend is getting hot and would like to see you in the parking lot *right now.*"

My attempt to put a light spin on a serious situation failed and 65,000 people hollered "Boo!" A wave of darkness rolled out of the crowd and onto the field. Competitors stopped playing. Frisbees fell to the ground. Everyone paused, waiting. I responded from pure instinct and called out to the crowd, "How many of you came here today to have a really good time?" The crowd yelled back "Yeah!" and the wave of darkness floated away. The dog lived to bark another day, and everyone was uplifted.

Guiding the energy of any group toward a constructive purpose is an essential form of service. This is true whether you are leading a team, focusing a department, building the culture of an entire organization, or contributing to the future of our global civilization.

In 1985, I started another company to connect people across cultures with long-standing histories of misunderstanding and mistrust. I organized Frisbee Friendship Tours to the People's Republic of China, was featured in *LIFE* magazine, guided Youth Ambassadors of America to the Soviet Union, and was interviewed on Chinese and Soviet TV. One member of the Soviet politburo understood what I was really doing—connecting people—so he sanctioned our gathering with children, clowns, and plastic flying discs in Moscow's heavily patrolled Red Square.

Through all these crazy events and years of ceaseless travel, another lesson emerged. For my curious gatherings to succeed,

I had to work with police and parks departments, radio stations, newspapers, commercial sponsors, Frisbee experts, novices, and even dogs. I had to figure out what each of these groups wanted to achieve and then design and deliver an event that gave each group what it valued.

> "I don't know what your destiny will be, but this I know: the only ones amongst you who will be truly happy are those who have sought and found a way to serve."
>
> *Albert Schweitzer,*
> *Nobel Prize winner*

Radio stations want interesting interviews. Sponsors need high visibility. Expert players enjoy good music and good crowds. Parks departments appreciate clean and safe events. Police insist on orderly traffic. Photographers seek "the shot" to capture the essence of the scene. Dogs need cool shade and clean water. *When each group gets what it really needs, and when all of us feel well served and understood, then everyone can be uplifted together.*

This lesson applies far beyond the Frisbee field. Whenever people with different interests meet in the fields of community or commerce, each of us makes a fundamental choice to focus first on what we want or on serving others. The surprising truth is this: the best way to get what you want in life is by helping others get what they want.

Surprising Singapore

In 1990, I went to Singapore for one week at the invitation of Singapore Airlines and the government's National Productivity Board. The country was seeking to transform from a low-cost manufacturing base to a value-adding center for services, ideas, and innovation. One week stretched into a month, then into a year, and now into more than two incredible decades.

During that time, I helped create a service curriculum for the nation, teaching thousands to create more value in the world and in their lives through service. I created the company UP! Your Service with its cheeky name to highlight three important points: *UP!* is the direction you'll travel to grow your income, your company, or your career. *Your* is a declaration of personal responsibility—this upward action must be taken by you. *Service* is your dedication to caring about other people, secure in the knowledge that you get more for yourself when you create for others what they appreciate, respect, and value.

Service industries have always been in my client list with Singapore Airlines, Raffles Hotel, and Changi Airport among the first distinguished organizations I served. Retail, hospitality, health care, insurance, finance, and real estate companies all appreciate the value of delivering great service. But there is also growing demand from the technology, telecommunications, pharmaceuticals, manufacturing, government, and other sectors. The value of service as a differentiator is especially high in industries in which products are easily commoditized and delivery is quickly matched.

Over the years, I have seen profound changes in people's attitudes and actions and dramatic improvements in many companies' service performance, with measurable gains in reputation, market share, and profits. Organizations that build vibrant and uplifting service cultures enjoy a sustainable competitive advantage, attracting and retaining better customers as well as more talented and motivated employees.

The Global Service Challenge

Two contradictory themes run throughout human history. One is the theme of misunderstanding: avoiding dialogue, accumulating mistrust, and armed conflict. The other is better understanding: creating dialogue, building new value, and accumulating trust. Selfishness and fear are at the root of the first, while compassion, generosity, and a commitment to serving others are at the heart of the latter. What causes someone to choose one path over the other? Why are some people so persistently caring and others so regularly rude? Why do some experience life as an ongoing opportunity, while others suffer it as a source of never-ending complaints? More importantly, how can we interrupt this pattern of conflict and missed opportunities to create better lives—and give our children a better future?

The challenge we face today is global in scale and scope: to bring a passion for uplifting service to every culture and corner of the world. The principles of delivering superior service should be taught in our schools, practiced in our communities, and woven into every fabric of our lives.

Years ago I made the decision to serve a larger social purpose. That desire has been at the core of my intentions and actions from organizing Frisbee festivals and international tours to designing and delivering service improvement and culture-building programs. I put my ideas and energy to work to promote the well-being of others. Now, you can do this, too.

We live in an extraordinary time. We have the technological and social ability to connect and serve each other as never before. Yes, there are many problems, but also breakthroughs. There are confused and dangerous individuals, but also many people acting with commitment, compassion, and concern.

I believe the readers of this book are people who enjoy making useful contributions. Whether you do this in your work and your community, or in your home and personal life, the service you provide to others creates a more enlightened planet for us all.

Thank you for reading and sharing this book and for putting what you learn into action. As you apply what you learn, other people will be uplifted in their lives, and you will be uplifted in yours.

I hope we have the privilege of meeting in person one day soon, and sharing the joy of uplifting service.

My warmest and best wishes to you,

Ron Kaufman

The Problem with Service Today

We are facing a crisis of service all over the world.

Huge economies are transforming from manufacturing-based to service-based at record speed, and our populations are largely unprepared. Customers are angry and complain to anyone who will listen. Service providers are irritated to the point of resentment and resignation. Countless organizations promise satisfaction to external customers and then allow internal politics to frustrate their employees' good intentions to deliver. And our early educational systems don't even recognize the subject of service as an area for serious study.

Yes, we face a service crisis. But, how can that be?

Service is present in every aspect of our lives from the moment we are born. We enter this world completely dependent on other people to serve us with food, clothing, shelter, medical care, education, and affection. Longer than any other species on earth, young people are dependent on constant service from parents, teachers, doctors, and community leaders.

As we grow, we go to work, become professionals, and get jobs, earning money and building our careers in successful service to others. When we become parents, we are service providers to the next generation. And when we become caregivers to our own parents, the roles are reversed and we are service providers to those who first served us.

We live and work in a world that is completely infused with service. In commerce this includes customer service and colleagues providing internal service. We have roadside service, desk-side service, counter service, delivery service, and self-service. In our communities we depend on the civil service, public service, government service, military service, and foreign service. When we gather to worship it's called a religious service, and when someone dies there is a memorial service.

Service is all around you; it's everywhere you look and live. But still, there is a vast disconnect between the high volume and the low quality of service we experience every day. In fact, there is a twofold catastrophe in our lives that makes very little sense. First, many individuals and organizations are unable to provide consistently satisfying service to customers, clients, and colleagues. And, second, many service providers complain continuously about jobs they dislike.

With service all around us, and so much a part of our daily lives, why aren't we doing it better? Why is service in this abysmal state? What is the problem? In fact, there are two problems.

Problem 1: Service Is Considered Servile

"The customer is king" implies the service provider is not. The word *serve* comes from the Latin word for "slave," which is hardly an attractive proposition. It's no wonder even the word *service* is avoided by many professionals. People want to be the boss, the leader, the manager, the rule maker—not the humble servant.

On a wider commercial scale, it doesn't help that the "customer service department" is often seen as a necessary evil, tacked on the end of a company value chain like the caboose on a train. It's the place people go only when things go wrong, where angry customers are seen and heard, where service providers toil until they can take no more, and where costs are to be cut, contained, and attributed to other company functions.

This outdated interpretation is operationally, economically, and emotionally counterproductive.

Numerous organizations and studies have proved that loyal customers are more profitable than customer churn and that better service is a key to retaining your best customers. Plus, the positioning of superior service allows for higher pricing and margins, and shareholder value tends to grow in step with a company's service reputation in the industry. Furthermore, when staff members are associated with an excellent service organization, their pride is measurable; employees are more engaged, more productive, and more committed to the organization. Uplifting service organizations simply attract, develop, and retain better talent. People want to work for, and want to be associated with, organizations that are distinguished by uplifting service.

With these benefits so recognized and clear, why is improving and sustaining great service so difficult to achieve? There is another problem.

Problem 2: The World of Service Is Poorly Mapped

Look into any field of human activity and you will find terms that people in that field use and understand. Doctors and nurses refer to systolic and diastolic pressures. Chefs and cooks use the terms *blanch* and *bottom cuts*. Carpenters work with trusses, joists, plumbs, and stringers. All well-developed areas of human activity feature recognized terms for commonly accepted ideas and principles in their fields. These are called *fundamental linguistic distinctions.*

But the world of service, and continuous service improvement, has no such common language. The whole domain suffers from weak clichés, poor distinctions, and inaccurate common sense. "The customer is always right" is often wrong. "Go the extra mile" is bad advice when the client wants precise fulfillment of exactly what was promised. "Serve others the way you would like to be served" is well-intentioned but misguided. Good service is not about what you like; it's about what someone else prefers. Service academics have created many meaningful terms: *gap models, channel preferences, promoter scores,* and more. But these have not become widely understood among the millions of service providers worldwide.

Well-developed domains of human activity also feature *standard practices* that deliver predictable and reliable results. Pilots land aircraft safely by adhering to carefully documented checklists. Accountants complete audits by following a step-by-step review of contracts, resolutions, and supporting documentation. Religious events follow time-honored routines and traditions. And sports teams compete within accepted rules of play.

A Confused Culture

But once again, the world of continuous service improvement—and building service culture—has struggled without a proven way of working. We have suffered from the lack of fundamental principles, effective processes, actionable models and frameworks to guide us successfully along the way.

So, What's the Solution?

First, we must transform the outdated view that service to others makes us subservient, subordinate, or servile. Service is taking action to create value for someone else. And that is the essence of every successful business, organization, and career. Uplifting service brings pride to service teams and increases service providers' sense of fulfillment and satisfaction at work. Uplifting service at home and in our communities makes our lives more enjoyable and rewarding. Far from subservience, providing uplifting service to others is the essential reason we are alive and here on earth together. Uplifting what you do for other people is the key to uplifting yourself.

Next, we need a proven path, a map, and a methodology that works with fundamental principles to apply in every service situation. We need practices that will consistently and reliably deliver service value in our professional and personal lives. We need a common service language to effectively communicate our visions, our expectations, and our promises to each other. We need to teach people to think about service not just as a procedure to follow, but as a mindset of purposeful engagement and proactive communication that leads to productive behavior. We need leaders who model service at every level of an organization. And, we need an architecture that helps any group of people engineer a self-sustaining culture of uplifting service. A passionate group of like-minded people with a plan and a commitment to action can and will transform our world.

Imagine that world right now. Imagine a world in which everyone is encouraged and encouraging. Imagine a world in which the common intention isn't just to resolve problems, but also to uplift and inspire others. Imagine a world in which people measure their success by the

An Aligned Culture

responses they receive, not by the actions they take. Imagine a workplace in which tasks and projects aren't considered complete until someone has been surprised or delighted. Imagine a world in which people are committed to uplifting the spirit and the practice of service because they really want to, not just because they were asked, ordered, or paid to. Finally, imagine an organization—your organization—truly uplifted, with every person fully engaged, encouraging each other, improving customer experience, making the company more successful, and contributing to the community at large.

What This Book Will Do for You

This book reveals the power of uplifting service and the steps you can take to build a sustainable culture that delivers it every day. This book answers questions about continuous service improvement and clears away many misconceptions. It spotlights companies and people all over the world who make service their top priority, enjoying great rewards and reputations. This book provides the insights you need to begin elevating your organization—and your own perspective.

This book will lead you on a proven path to truly uplifting service. This path works whether you serve external customers or internal colleagues, individually or as part of a team, in any function and at any level inside an organization. The tools and practices in this book have been proven effective in every context you can imagine: in business, government, communities, and homes; on every continent; and in many languages.

All over the world, people like you are taking practical steps to understand their customers better, create more positive experiences, generate greater value, deepen loyalty, and build longer-term relationships for the future. All over the world, people are also looking for new ways to enjoy their work more fully, to get along with colleagues more easily, and to feel better about their customers and about themselves. The pathway to achieving these important professional and personal goals is through providing more uplifting service.

By taking the steps presented in this book, you will earn greater success in your business and enjoy more fulfillment in your life. You will feel better about the people you are serving and the person you are becoming.

Welcome to the new world of uplifting service.

SECTION ONE

WHY?

CHAPTER 1

Journey into a New Culture

It was the opportunity he had waited a lifetime for—traveling across the ocean to discover a new world, and a new way of conducting business. So, there he sat, staring into the darkness while his family slept in a nearby room, his bag packed with the only suit he owned resting at his feet. He flipped through the empty pages of his passport while he waited. Finally, headlights appeared in the driveway, creeping slowly toward the house.

Of course, this opportunity made the young man's family proud, especially his wife—even though she was staying home with their young children and would wait anxiously for his return. It made his father proud, who had worked so hard to give his son a better life than his own. And this opportunity made the young man's mother proud, as she believed from the day he was born that her son was destined for better things.

In the car on the way to the airport, the young man recalled his simple childhood—frigid mornings warming his hands by a woodburning stove. He remembered the family gatherings when generations would mingle, sharing stories and family legends, and sitting in his small schoolroom daydreaming about new worlds.

As the car entered the big city, the young man noticed people glaring, with poverty in their eyes. He passed storefronts spray-painted with graffiti and with windows clad with thin steel bars, the only barrier between shopkeepers and thieves. In one tattered storefront window, a sign screamed out, "SELLING EVERY-THING! GOING OUT OF BUSINESS AFTER 40 YEARS."

"Sad," the young man thought. "Where did the prosperity go?"

The airport was congested and cluttered. Car horns honked. People scurried. Buses barged their way into the pandemonium. It was a madhouse. The taxi driver stopped far before the entrance and said, "You'll have to walk. I'm not wasting my time in that mess."

Inside the airport, passengers crowded into lines that stretched through narrow, seemingly endless hallways. The young man hadn't even left his native country yet, but he felt consumed by anarchy—the polite civilian nature of his youth squashed by the harsh reality of tough economic times. Travelers rudely fought for a spot in line at the gate. Everyone was anxious.

Agents and employees at the airport were also sharp. It seemed their primary concern was to simply herd people through as quickly as possible, repeating their mantra, "Keep it moving." The young man let the agents direct him and kept his mind focused on the task at hand—leaving this chaos behind for the learning experience of his lifetime.

"You!" screamed the gate agent, pointing at the young man and waving him over abruptly. "Give me your papers." And so, the young man did, realizing that he would let nothing get in the way of his boarding the airplane. He didn't care how rudely he was treated, how long he had to stand in line, how hard he needed to work to keep his composure, or how assertive he needed to be to claim his turn. This was the kind of turmoil and disarray the young man hoped would not exist in the new world. And although he had heard stories, he could not help but wonder, "Does such a new world and a more considerate culture really exist?"

"Whatever happened to the ideology of respect?" the young man wondered quietly. "What happened to human generosity and compassion?" He remembered the kind, helpful man who owned a small grocery store in the town where he grew up. He remembered his mother's unwavering loyalty and how she would not shop for groceries anywhere else. He smiled as he remembered the years he worked in that store after school, helping customers, carrying bags, and smiling with his colleagues as they brought groceries and smiles to everyone else.

"Your flight is boarding," said the gate agent loudly, snapping the young man out of his reverie. The young man stood in line until it was his turn at the counter. He watched as the agent checked his name, Todd Nordstrom, on his passport and boarding pass. Todd walked onto the plane in silence.

Unlike so many stories through the ages, in which young people from less-developed parts of the world travel westward to Europe and North America in search of a better life, this story follows a new tide that's turning in the other direction. Twenty-one hours after leaving North America behind, the airplane touched down and the doors opened. A waft of fresh air filled the cabin, and this young man stepped into the new world.

He had heard the stories, but the reality overwhelmed him. This airport didn't resemble anything he had ever seen before. The ceilings were as high as the sky. And although it was the middle of the night, the building was lit to appear as if it were the middle of the day. The walkways were wide enough to be roadways, and they were clean—not a trace of litter. Lush plants and flowers enveloped ponds where exotic fish swam. Families gathered and posed for photographs. As his eyes and ears filled with wonder, Todd found smiles greeting him at every turn.

"Welcome, sir," said an airport employee. "May I help you find something?"

"I just got off the airplane," Todd replied.

The airport employee chuckled. "You must be tired," he said. "Where did you come from?"

"America," he said. "I flew in from Los Angeles."

The airport employee grinned and noticed a luggage tag hanging from his bag. "Welcome to Singapore, Mr. Nordstrom. We are glad you are here."

In Search of Uplifting Service

This Mr. Nordstrom isn't related to the iconic retailer that shares his name—a profitable retail brand often used to illustrate the power of excellent customer service. In fact, he is not an expert in customer service at all. He's a friend of mine, a typical young businessman, curious about achieving success. He's curious to know how others have made it happen. His views of the world are limited only by what he already knows.

I invited Todd to visit me in Singapore to experience firsthand what I have learned in this country and in other locations all over the world. I wanted to show him what was possible—and to change his perceptions forever.

This is not a book of heartwarming stories of fantastic customer service at The Ritz-Carlton, Disney, or Singapore Airlines. These iconic service providers have earned and deserve their prestige and commercial success. But service is not merely the act of treating customers well. There is a greater definition and a greater role for service to play in your life, and in our world. This book will show you how to create that world.

What is the real definition of service? What does it mean to create a service culture? What are the benefits—for customers, colleagues, and communities—of building an uplifting service culture? And, most importantly, what actions can you take right now to bring these benefits to your life?

All of these questions will be answered throughout this book. And, although you may think you already know the answers, you'll be surprised by what you learn and delighted with what you discover. You'll see how service has become diluted to the dull cliché we call "customer service." And, you'll realize that global businesses, communities, governments, and humankind in general are just now witnessing the birth of our true service potential.

Service is not just a reaction to a request. It's not a department that responds to complaints. Service is not a company policy. It's not a standard procedure.

Service is greater than that—it's a gateway to fulfillment, satisfaction, and delight. It's a curiosity to listen intently and appreciate others, a commitment to taking action and creating value. Service is a contribution affecting every business, industry, culture, and person—including you. To see the true impact of uplifting service, we need to look farther than over the counter, over the web, or over the phone. We need to look for examples and insights all over the world.

Why Service? Why Singapore?

Singapore is a unique and extraordinary island south of China. It's small—about 280 square miles of landmass, with fewer than 6 million residents, and less than an hour-long drive from coast to coast. Yet the country is one of the leading financial centers in the world. It hosts one of the busiest shipping ports in the world. Year after year it's rated one of the best places to live and conduct business. It has held the rank of fastest-growing economy in the world, and has yet to celebrate its 50th birthday.

The principal gateway to Singapore is the airport. It's no ordinary airport. In fact, it is the most awarded airport in the world, and it has an extraordinary impact on the entire country.

How can an airport have so much impact—especially on a nation with such high credentials? Backtrack to Singapore in the early 1990s and you'll notice a very different picture of the country. Singapore has few natural resources other than its people and its strategic location. In the 1980s and 1990s, the manufacturing base of the country was moving to China where land was vast and labor inexpensive. Administrative tasks were being outsourced to India and other low-cost locations. Singapore's educational system was focused on supporting the manufacturing base with quality-assurance training and business models.

Singapore could see the opportunity in service-based industries like medical, financial, legal, education, hospitality, entertainment, and retail, but the nation's human resources hadn't developed to support these service industries. The people of Singapore had been educated to know the answer, pass the test, do the right thing (the first time), avoid making mistakes, and follow proven procedures. But to serve? What does that mean in a culture in which everyone is meticulously trained to reliably follow the rules?

This challenge went even deeper. Singapore has a global reputation for vigorous law enforcement. It is, quite possibly, one of the safest places in the world—unless you're a criminal. Singapore had developed a stable culture of law-abiding citizens. So how can people educated to explicitly follow rules and regulations adapt to roles that require adaptation, creativity, and problem solving every day?

Singapore had to transform an entire nation that knew how to follow instructions well, but was hesitant to follow a customer wherever their interests may have led. Government officials recognized this conundrum. Yet, they also realized the opportunity—and the necessity—to transform. In fact, driven by the vision of the country's founding prime minister, Mr. Lee Kuan Yew, government leaders have been guiding this country through successful transformations from the beginning. Today, as many parts of the world struggle with deep challenges and difficult change, this small country is a unique example to study. Singapore offers a wide range of successful organizations, uplifting service experiences, and practical insights for enduring success.

When Singapore claimed independence in 1965, it was a time of racial tension and economic hardship. In a land populated by immigrants with a potentially volatile mix of ethnicities, religions, and economic backgrounds, the population and the law had to respect social differences and allow (if not demand) economic progress. That was an all-embracing and law-abiding transformation.

The country's geographic location made it a port of constant commerce, bringing travelers and companies from all parts of the globe to engage in business, enjoy leisure, or simply connect in transit to another part of the world. But Singapore wanted to become a premier global hub for creating and exchanging value, not just an exotic local bazaar, a transit point, or an interesting regional destination. To find its place in the wider world, Singapore had to undergo another enormous change of thinking and global understanding throughout the nation.

Then, during the 1990s and into the next century, as Singapore's low-cost economy disappeared and value-adding services took root, the time for another transformation had come, a transformation of thinking and action to create even greater value for people throughout the world—and for the people of Singapore— a transformation of attitudes from command to creativity and of behaviors from compliance and control to concern and compassion. In short, an *uplifting service* transformation.

If you want to transform a mindset, convert an industrial base, inspire a diverse amalgamation of people, and uplift an entire nation, where do you start? You start at the gateway. You start at the airport.

Changi Airport's "Why?"

Singapore realized something that much of the rest of the world is still trying to figure out—there is a service crisis in the world, and only focused attention and persistently positive action are going to fix it. Businesses have turned a very simple human concept into a catastrophic cliché. Bosses demand "customer service" from frontline employees as if it were a performance metric. They remain blind to the fact that true service comes not from demands and dashboards, but from a basic human desire to take care of other people. So many organizations, rooted in task and efficiency metrics of the industrial revolution, have stuffed the concept of service into disconnected departments and filled it with meaningless mantras and reactionary rhetoric, without stopping to realize its true potential.

"Oh, you want service?" an employee asks. "Well, you'll have to talk to our service department." Or, "You want something else or something different? That's not our policy." "It's not my job to make you happy," says a manager. "Talk to human resources if you've got something to say." An executive might even say, "It's not personal. It's just business."

What happens to customers' loyalty when they realize that some employees are not concerned with achieving or delivering their satisfaction? What happens to team members when their manager is unwilling to help support or serve their needs? And what happens to an organization that isn't concerned about the welfare of its employees, its community, its industry, or its social contribution? Morale declines, performance suffers, and service spirals further downward.

Where does service really start? And where does it end? In Singapore, it starts when and where you land—at the gateway.

Since the airport's humble beginnings in 1981, Changi Airport has evolved to become a global standard of functionality, aesthetics, and service. It is currently the world's seventh-busiest airport, serving, surprising, and delighting more than 42 million travelers a year—that's more than seven times larger than Singapore's entire population.

The airport property is nothing short of exceptional. It's jammed with amenities unseen at any other airport in the world, like a butterfly garden, outdoor swimming pool, playground equipment, a four-story slide, napping rooms, spa treatments, and entertainment venues that include movie theaters, multimedia and online experiences, and even video-gaming stations.

Sounds like a great time, right? It is. However, it's much more than some fun between flights. The stress-free atmosphere of Changi Airport is a soothing oasis where you can relax, regroup, and reclaim your senses. It's a chance to reconnect with loved ones, call home, or meet someone new. It's a place where you can find yourself, and be yourself.

In the same way, Singapore is a place in which the world can see itself, too. It's an entire country in just one city. It's a wide range of races, religions, and cultures all serving each other and succeeding together. It's a small country in a big region serving customers from all over the world. It's a mix of people and languages using a commitment to uplifting service to build a better future. Singapore is a microcosm of the world. What works in this country can work in your company, your organization, your career, and your life. Uplifting service can work in your world, too.

The Adventure That Lies Ahead

With each chapter of this book, you will take another step on the proven path into a world where service has the power to uplift, delight, and inspire.

We'll start inside Changi Airport and discover *why* Singapore embraced uplifting service at this important gateway.

Then we will travel inside the infrastructure of two other Singapore-based organizations, NTUC Income and Marina Bay Sands. The former is the nation's largest insurance company whose mission and vision of service are unique. The latter is a new, integrated resort on a journey to global magnificence, accelerating its business performance and enabling human potential with an uplifting service culture.

We'll leave Singapore to visit uplifting service organizations and destinations around the globe—Nokia Siemens Networks (now NSN) with telecommunications customers in more than 100 countries; Royal Vopak based in Holland with a global span of oil storage and chemical handling facilities; Xerox in the United Arab Emirates; and Wipro, an IT and consulting powerhouse based in India and serving clients worldwide with a customer-centric competitive edge.

Uplifting service transforms individuals, teams, and entire organizations. I've witnessed its power and its impact firsthand. And along the way, I've gathered insights, interviews, best practices, and strategies from the world's most successful service cultures, innovators, and leaders. You will meet these leaders and discover the challenges they have overcome and the rewards they have achieved. And, for the first time, the essential architecture they use to engineer an uplifting service culture will be revealed so that you can use it, too.

Uplifting service is not just a business mantra; it's a transformational mindset. It's a powerful driver of engagement, loyalty, and trust. It's an accelerant, a connector, and a movement. And it's the only aspect of business that fuels and feeds the spirit of every person to create a sustainable advantage, a continuous improvement, and a constant uplifting of people's performance, passion, and potential.

Like Todd Nordstrom's view of the world and service after he visited me in Singapore, your understanding and perception are about to change forever.

CHAPTER 2

The Gateway
to Possibility

It was 9 p.m. in Minnesota. It was January, and the temperature was 22 degrees below zero—a bone-chilling reminder of Mother Nature's occasional cruelty. Most people were warm and safe at home, cuddling up in front of a movie. Unless, of course, there was something more intriguing to discover.

Four teenagers ignored the bitter cold that night. They were in the car together, on a life-changing journey. One of them, 16-year-old Amanda, was a good student and a cheerleader. She was anxious because her friends were pressuring her to do something she had never done before, something she didn't understand. "You've got to try it," they said. "Everyone cool does it."

They pulled into a dimly lit parking lot. Amanda took a deep breath and followed her friends into an unfamiliar place, surprisingly full of people, where she quickly found solace by standing behind her friends in a line. They began using words that she didn't understand, and she was terrified when her turn came. "This is my first time," she said. "I don't know what I'm supposed to do."

The young man facing her smiled. "Well, then, let me be the first to welcome you to Starbucks."

Amanda has been a Starbucks Coffee superfan ever since that fateful night. A decade later, she can still be found sipping hot coffee inside her neighborhood Starbucks—a notion she once found odd. Young people drink coffee? Who drinks coffee at night anyway? Apparently, a lot of people do.

But it wasn't the caffeine that attracted her—Amanda prefers decaffeinated coffee. Starbucks hooked Amanda on something else. It is well documented that the company's founders wanted to create a place for conversation and a sense of community, a third place where their customers could relax and connect outside of home and work. They created a spot with an inviting ambience, comfortable seating, a hip vibe, and great (but not too loud) music. It would be the perfect place to enjoy a conversation, read a book, or do some work with a delicious drink to keep you going. That experience is what keeps customers coming back to Starbucks. But the intrigue that pulls people through the door their very first time is not the Starbucks experience. It's not the coffee. It's not even the hype. It's bigger than that. It's Starbucks' uplifting answer to this essential question, "Why?"

"Why?" is a powerful question in the human psyche. It opens up new perspectives and new possibilities for individuals, businesses, governments, and the entire human race. It's a powerful question that allows us to analyze the reason, explore the purpose, or discover the deeper cause. It is a gateway to learning how to grow, achieve, motivate, differentiate, find a position, take a position, or discover a purpose. Without asking the question, "Why?" some gates never open.

Again consider Changi Airport—why build a butterfly garden? I don't think an airport employee opened the suggestion box one day to find the request, "I would really like to see shorter lines, faster luggage handling, more taxis, and a butterfly garden." Yet, Changi Airport built one of the most delightful butterfly gardens in the world, with a profusion of flowering plants, lush greenery, and an indoor waterfall. Airport visitors can witness the beauty of not just a few butterflies, but hundreds. Stand still for just a moment and a butterfly will settle on your shoulder, its delicate wings caressing you with color. It's breathtaking.

Butterflies in an Airport?

"Why butterflies?" Todd Nordstrom asked me as we toured around Changi Airport.

I couldn't help but smile at his question. "Why a swimming pool? Why a four-story slide?" I replied. "These are all something personal, delightful, and surprising."

He stood speechless.

"Do you realize how deep your question is?" I asked him. "How are you feeling about this airport right now? How are you feeling about the people who work here and about Singapore?" He took a deep, slow breath, and as he relaxed, a smile spread across his face.

Consider how delightful service makes you feel. Consider how it feels to have an associate in a retail store pay close attention just to you. Consider how it feels when an auto mechanic goes out of his way to help save you money or when a banker takes the time to really explain the differences between accounts, services, and fees. Consider how it feels when a colleague listens carefully to completely understand your request and then gives you exactly what you need.

"Why?"

Why do Nordstrom stores have live pianists playing grand pianos? Why does Google allow its employees to ride scooters in the workplace or feed them with a fantastic array of free food? Why does New Belgium Brewing in Colorado, brewer of Fat Tire beer, offer incentives to employees who ride their bikes, walk, or jog to work? Why does Microsoft send key employees to work full-time for months in charitable organizations while keeping them on the company payroll?

All of these are service initiatives—focused on serving a different audience. They target customers, employees, the community, or the environment. But, why serve others? Why focus your attention and your actions on the needs, desires, preferences, and curiosities of other people?

It's simple. Service creates value that extends in all directions. Uplifting service uplifts everyone.

The Gateway: Why Uplifting Service?

"Our vision is to connect lives," says Changi Airport's Executive Vice President of Airport Management, Mr. Foo Sek Min. "Airports are typically stressful places. Our goal is to remove that stress. Our culture of service must envelop all the 200 organizations operating here. Everyone's experience with the service we provide to passengers must be aligned, the people, the process, even the equipment."

Mr. Foo isn't just talking about connecting people, processes, and equipment at the airport. He's talking about connecting people, processes, and equipment to a bigger purpose, a greater reason, and a deeper cause. He's talking about connecting people to the country of Singapore and connecting Singapore to people and organizations from many other places. The employees at Changi Airport are connected. The customers are connected. The country is connected. And that's valuable in every direction—for everyone.

This may seem ideological. It may even seem unattainable to many people and organizations. And many companies will view the Changi Airport service mentality as something indulgent or outrageous, saying, "That would never work for us."

"Why?"

Everyone has a past to overcome or a current "this is how we always do it" attitude to move beyond. Due to Singapore's reputation for strict law enforcement, it had earned the nickname "Singabore." But look at the country today—the entire community is breaking the molds of sterile process and bureaucratic service. In fact, it's become an international phenomenon. Uplifting service is the essence of the country's commercial culture and its contribution. Singapore's passion is to create and innovate, to constantly find new ways to upgrade and uplift the nation's service to the world.

But Singapore is not the only game changer. Zappos wasn't the first company to sell shoes online, but because of its reputation for zany yet sincere customer service, it's captured the world spotlight. Starbucks certainly wasn't the first unique coffee shop, yet other companies have tried to imitate the Starbucks experience time and again. And, although Disney wasn't the first amusement park, it is often the first company that comes to mind for children and families around the world.

Companies and organizations can break away and change the status quo by asking and answering three powerful questions that all begin with "Why?" Why improve your service? Why build a service culture? Why build an uplifting service culture that upgrades performance and profit while uplifting the spirits of everyone involved—customers, colleagues, and even whole communities?

The big opportunity isn't just to understand other companies' reasons, purposes, or causes. It's to figure out your reasons, your purpose, and your cause—to start your own service revolution right where you are.

Are you attempting to overcome a specific hurdle? Are you trying to attract, engage, and keep great employees? Are you seeking a sustainable commercial advantage? Are you trying to delight your customers, your colleagues, and maybe even yourself?

What's your gateway to new possibilities? Why will employees, investors, vendors, community members, and customers all be drawn to your allure?

Why Improve Your Service?

I define *service* this way:

Service is taking action to create value for someone else.

These are simple yet powerful words. Still, they leave a gray area for interpretation about whether the service is good or not, whether the value is high or low. A carpet cleaning company provides a service. Of course, that doesn't mean it provides a good service. At minimum, you expect dirt to be removed from your carpet. If its employees don't remove the dirt, we say the company didn't provide the service. Eventually, no one wants to hire that company and it goes out of business.

But if the same company goes above and beyond your expectations—to surprise you and delight you—then customers say it's a great service provider. Eventually, more people talk about the company, buy services from it, and look forward to interacting with it. As its service reputation grows, its business also grows stronger.

It's shortsighted, however, to view service only in terms of business transactions, colleagues, and customers. A friend provides the service of friendship. A mother serves her daughter. An employee provides service to his or her employer. A company can serve the community. Government provides service to the people. A nation can provide service to other nations. The list goes on, and in every situation mentioned, the roles of service recipient and service provider could be exchanged. These are all service relationships with value flowing in both directions.

The point is this: we all come into this world depending on other people to take care of us, to serve us. As we grow, other people depend on us to serve them. We all receive service and provide service just to stay alive.

So, why service? It's a necessity. You might even say, as I do, that service is the reason we are here.

Why Build a Service Culture?

Whether you realize it or not, you participate in a collection of service cultures. The question is: what do your service cultures look, sound, and feel like?

On the most basic level, a service culture means that everyone in your team, your group, or your company shares a set of attitudes, goals, and practices that characterize the value you offer and the way you deliver your service. If you're a carpet cleaning company, is your team simply focused on getting out the dirt? Or is everyone dedicated to making your company the preferred carpet cleaner? If the former, you get the job done as quickly as you can, and then you get out. If the latter, you offer tips and suggestions, put furniture back in its original position, and maybe even roll out a small red carpet when your client inspects the work you have performed.

The point is that your team's shared attitudes, goals, and practices characterize the value of the service you provide and define your service culture today.

Why Build an Uplifting Service Culture?

In an uplifting service culture, people gain a deeper understanding of themselves, their purpose, their relationships, and their possibilities for today and for the future. This is where individuals and organizations can realize their full potential.

An uplifting service culture is one in which the character and value of the service you provide elevates and inspires you—and uplifts the people around you. It elevates standards, attitudes, and expectations, uplifting the perceptions, practices,

22

processes, and products of employees and leaders, colleagues and customers, vendors, partners, regulators, suppliers, and whole communities—everyone touched by and therefore contributing to the culture.

And here's the best part about building an uplifting service culture: it's not a destination. It's forever changing and evolving, an organic phenomenon in which all the people, practices, and processes can drive performance even higher, reaching for—and achieving—ever higher potential.

It's Changi Airport acting as the gateway to Singapore with spas and slides and butterflies showing the country and the world what's possible every day. It's Zappos and its zany behavior capturing media attention, energizing employees to even more outrageous acts of service, capturing even more attention, and ultimately attracting more customers. It's Disney's commitment to give each visitor the experience of a lifetime. It's Google providing its employees with outside-the-box creative time and workspaces—allowing their minds to explore uncharted worlds and then create world-changing online tools. It's your neighborhood baker who saves leftover donut holes and delivers them to the nearby orphanage. It's a daughter raising money door-to-door for the breast cancer volunteer association, walking 60 miles to help save the life of a woman she doesn't know, because her own mother died from the disease years before. It's a boy on the street picking up a piece of trash someone else dropped. And it's a gentleman holding the door open, not for a beautiful woman, but for anyone—because uplifting service is a beautiful experience for everyone.

We all serve, and must be served, to survive. Then we are all already members of a global service culture. But, until we define the value that our service and our culture will contribute in this world—until we make a deliberate commitment to elevate our own expectations, goals, and standards—we allow uplifting possibilities to pass.

If we want to grow, evolve, and progress in this world—as individuals, as communities, or as a global human civilization—we must ask ourselves this question every day: Why?

Why serve others? To get what you need or want? Why improve your service? To get more business, or stay in business? Or to contribute to the welfare and well-being of others?

Why contribute to a service culture? To earn a bonus or a promotion? To earn a higher margin, or enjoy a better reputation? Or to enjoy working more each day with your customers and colleagues?

Why build an uplifting service culture? To stand out from the crowd, or attract a bigger crowd? To care more deeply for the lives of your customers, the spirit of your colleagues, and the well-being of your community? Or to build a stronger and more uplifting spirit of service into the core of your team, your business, and yourself?

Are You Ready?

There are thought leaders and business leaders in the world today who have answered these questions with inspiring intentions and impressive results. What have they declared? What have they created? How did they build inspiring and continuously uplifting service cultures?

It wasn't by chance or by luck, and it wasn't by personal charisma. They used a proven architecture to build some of the finest service cultures in the world today. And now, you can use it, too.

Are you ready to create your own gateway to uplifting service? Are you ready for a world-changing butterfly experience where you work and live?

Let's take the next step together. Turn the page.

CHAPTER 3

The Proven Path

When he was just nine years old, a boy migrated with his family from Lithuania to Cape Town, South Africa, in hope of a better life. He was a sports enthusiast, playing soccer, swimming, and lifting weights. His story seemed destined for an uplifting ending—a gutsy young person who overcomes adversity to change the world. Without a doubt, Louis Washkansky did make a contribution to our lives, but not in the manner you might expect.

When he was old enough, Louis joined the military, served during wartime, and then became a local grocer. But Louis' health declined sharply during middle age. He became a diabetic and, suffering from heart disease, survived three heart attacks. His third heart attack led Louis to Groote Schuur Hospital in South Africa, where doctors patiently explained that his congestive heart failure was untreatable. He was going to die fairly soon, and there was little, if anything, the doctors could do to save him.

Louis was willing to try anything to save his life. There was one radical new procedure the doctors wanted to attempt. It was his only chance at survival, but carried a devastating level of risk. The procedure was invasive and long, and it had never been done before. Louis agreed, and initially the procedure worked. He survived the surgery but died 18 days later from double pneumonia because of a weakened immune system.

Despite what it may seem, this wasn't a failure but the beginning of one of the medical profession's most dramatic advancements and innovations. This is the story of the first human heart transplant, performed by Dr. Christiaan Barnard.

The "why" in this story was obvious to both the patient and the doctors. The goal and challenge were clear. And the need for speed was urgent. The only thing not yet clear was "how." Dr. Barnard had a theory of what might work based on research and other organ transplant procedures. Yet, this was the first human heart transplant, and Barnard knew that Louis Washkansky, like every human, was unique. There was potential, and there would be problems.

This heart transplant procedure has been fine-tuned and practically perfected since the 1960s. A very specific plan now exists to guide surgeons to successfully transplant a human heart from a cadaver into the chest of a living human being. Yet, the most important hurdle that must always be respected—and for which the procedure must be adjusted every time—is the unique presenting condition of each patient.

The same is true when an organization aims to build an uplifting service culture. Every organization is different. The service history, attributes, customer expectations, competition, and industry regulations will vary immensely from one organization to the next. A financial services company like Singapore's NTUC Income can't build a winning service reputation by mimicking the zany antics of America's Zappos. It wouldn't make sense for

Wipro, one of the world's largest information technology services companies, to build a butterfly garden in its corporate headquarters like Changi Airport. Even in the same industry, the playfully profitable culture of budget carrier Southwest doesn't match the luxuriously profitable culture of Singapore Airlines.

Yet when we distill what each of these companies has done to build their distinctive service culture, a clear map emerges revealing a remarkably common, practical, and successful approach. There is a proven architecture and a roadmap for engineering an uplifting service culture that the world's service leaders have been using for years. It works in every industry and geography. It works in high tech and high touch, in education, in professional services and industry associations, and even in government organizations.

And now, I am bringing to you this same proven approach to build a distinctive and uplifting service culture in your team, your organization, your community, and your world.

A Prescription That Works

"This is unreal," said Todd Nordstrom, poking his head into the movie theater at Changi Airport. "Why would anyone want to get on their next flight? You could hang out here all day. This isn't an airport; it's an adventure."

He paused, letting his eyes follow many travelers as they wandered through the colorful terminal building. Then he took a deep breath and sighed. "It's too bad all businesses can't offer phenomenal experiences like this. I mean, sure, a motivated company can provide great service, but not like this with all the beautiful architecture and incredible amenities."

Again, I smiled. "Actually, the Changi Airport culture shares exactly the same uplifting service architecture as many other leading organizations. Yes, every company is different, and every industry and culture has their own unique ways of doing business. I've been helping leaders transform their service cultures for more than 25 years, and the situations they face are different, but the architecture they apply to build an uplifting service culture is exactly the same."

This architecture is a prescription that works. It's a proven design, a way of engineering teams and activities, and creating the future. It's a proven path for people like you and organizations like yours to consistently delight your customers, your colleagues, and everyone else you meet.

An Uplifting Service Architecture

A heart transplant has become a common practice, as do many endeavors after years of trial and error. Sony created the portable cassette tape player, and now music moves with no tape at all. American Express pioneered safe payments on the road with traveler's checks. Today payments are made quickly and easily through many mediums worldwide. Following directions with a printed map has become the GPS app on your smartphone.

But when it comes to building a uniquely strong service culture, the path to success has been less clear. It seems more anecdotal, dependent on the passion of a team or some founder's personality, and therefore less predictable or precise. At least that's what many believe.

Across two decades of experience with large and diverse organizations, I've had the privilege to gain insights and build solutions with some of the world's great service leaders. Over time I noticed a common framework that described and defined their actions. Although each organization was different, their circumstances varied, and although their answer to "Why service?" was not the same, their "How?" was remarkably consistent.

This insight led me to deeper research to analyze the organizations' common paths. It led me to ask many more questions of the organizations I worked with, about their past programs, their present actions, and their intended future. It led me to explore various angles and approaches from which an uplifting service culture could be conceived and successfully constructed. Ultimately, it led me to write this book, revealing the five key elements of an Uplifting Service Architecture that have proven effective and efficient over time.

WHY · LEAD · BUILD · LEARN · DRIVE

The Five Key Elements of an Uplifting Service Architecture

These five elements may appear simple, but understanding and making each an area of deep focus will be critical to your service success. Through this book, I will focus on each area in detail. And, I will ask you to take practical action steps in each area so you can build or improve your service culture right away.

1. Start with "Why?"

The previous chapter focused on three questions: Why improve your service? Why build a service culture? Why build an uplifting service culture?

These questions are powerful tools. It is vital that each person and team in your organization thinks about these questions carefully and answers them in detail. The three questions initiate reflection, consideration, and consolidation of ideas, leading to clear and well-defined goals.

Consider Xerox in the United Arab Emirates as an example for the first question. The massive document management company had an aggressive four-year goal to double in size, growing faster than the market while also increasing profit margins. They used excellent service as a key differentiator in the competitive marketplace and achieved their goals in spite of economic turmoil that upended all of their plans.

"The results speak for themselves: year-to-date revenue growth of 32%, 53% gross profit growth, and 52% net profit growth," said General Manager Andrew Hurt, 10 months into one of the most financially difficult years the world has ever seen.

Those are impressive results for an aggressive economic answer to the fundamental question, "Why improve your service?"

Your company may have a very different answer. Maybe you want to improve employee engagement, build teamwork across silos, or attract and retain better talent. Maybe you want to increase your top-line revenue, bottom-line profits, or add more value to your shareholders. Maybe you want to differentiate and stand above the competition by adding more value through your service, or your expanding range of services. Maybe you want to achieve a sustainable competitive advantage by building an uplifting service culture that delivers all of the above.

Whatever you decide, you will only find your answers when you and your team dedicate time to ask and answer the three major questions in the first section of this book.

2. Take the Lead

Uplifting service cultures are not built on strict policies dictated by leaders or by procedures controlled by managers. Instead, these cultures grow when *creating more value through better service* becomes the shared purpose within every aspect of your business, your interactions, and your transactions—from your boardroom all the way to your front lines.

Consider Parkway Health, a leading healthcare provider with 16 hospitals and 3,400 beds throughout Asia. According to CEO and Managing Director Dr. Tan See Leng, "We can have the best medical technology and facilities, but patients will not return if the service is poor." He's right. So Parkway Health deployed a top-down and bottom-up approach to improving service organization-wide—building fundamental service principles into the hospital operating system, sending all leaders, managers, and department heads through intensive service education, and certifying course leaders to spread the same message of uplifting service to every frontline staff member throughout the organization.

This coordinated campaign has enabled the growing company to view service challenges and new opportunities in a common way, yet from different levels and functional points of view. And because this initiative was promoted, supported, and launched at the same time from the top down and the bottom up, the company has demonstrated that it is possible for team members to lead service improvement from any position and at all levels.

We will explore this topic with examples and action steps you can take in the second section of the book, chapters 4 through 6.

3. Build with the Blocks

Of course, every organization is unique and structured differently. Nevertheless, successful service cultures share a similar structural focus when it comes to building an uplifting service culture. I call these "The 12 Building Blocks." Some of the blocks in your organization may already be in place. Some may be weak and need extra attention. Others may not need attention now but will in the future, or vice versa. The goal, as in any architectural or engineering endeavor, is to prioritize and then strategically organize your activities and building blocks to eliminate weakness, while leveraging strength.

Microsoft is an intriguing example of this challenge in action. The company provides software to billions of customers and works with a network of more than 700,000 developers and partners. Microsoft has very strong building blocks to support an ongoing stream of new product and service launches. But even Microsoft understands the need to improve its customers' and partners' experiences (CPE). CPE is a work in progress at Microsoft, as it requires a shift in the long-standing developer-centric and features-oriented culture. Instead of product groups and business units rapidly launching products and then improving customer experience by reacting to feedback, Microsoft is putting in place new activities to build a more proactive and collaborative culture, enabling employees to reach across silos and across the company to create the next great experience together.

By contrast, at Singapore Airlines, activities in all 12 Building Blocks have been developed, aligned, and fine-tuned since 1969 into an art form that delivers extraordinary service and profits. This world-class service culture consistently delivers in a global industry routinely plagued by complaints of cancelled flights, inconsistent service, and unstable financial performance.

You will learn more about the strategy and techniques of both these companies, and many more from around the world, in the third section of the book, chapters 7 through 18.

4. Learn to Improve

Just as reading every diet book in the store won't make you lose weight, simply reading about service won't improve your service performance or your culture unless you actually change your behaviors. Real service education means that people learn to think and act differently in service so that their actions always create value for someone else. To achieve this throughout an organization requires a Common Service Language based on fundamental service principles that apply to all internal and external service providers, at all levels, and in every business unit, department, or division. But lessons aren't enough. There must also be exercises customized for the service situations facing each service provider, and then wide-scale buy-in across the organization for the attitude and practices of uplifting service.

Look at Nokia Siemens Networks. This proud European company serves telecommunications providers and partners around the globe with more than 60,000 employees spread across 150 countries. "Today, everyone has access to the same information," said the company's CEO, Mr. Rajeev Suri. "Technology is outdated faster than ever before and competitors can replicate everything except our attitude, and our service-focused actions.

A superior service culture is what will distinguish us from the competition."

How do you educate a company of this size to take new action? In less than 24 months, Nokia Siemens Networks sent 650 members of its Executive Board and Global Leadership Team to service leadership workshops held in 14 cities around the world. Nokia Siemens Networks carefully selected and trained an elite group of 150 employees to become course leaders, who then taught a curriculum of world-class service education to more than 20,000 of their colleagues in less than 24 months. And they did this in 12 languages, creating a Common Service Language that works across the company and around the world.

This proven curriculum of world-class service education is given to you—with exercises you can use right away—in the fourth section of the book, chapters 19 through 24.

5. Drive Forward

Imagine hopping on a bicycle, cranking the pedals, and just when you start accelerating down a steep hill, you close your eyes and take your hands off the handlebars. It's crazy, I know. Yet, this is how many organizations approach new initiatives. They crank hard at the beginning, and then they let go. But leaders and organizations with successful service cultures don't let go—they hold on; they keep on cranking; they drive. Their eyes sparkle with the excitement of uplifting service goals. Their feet are firmly planted in the realities of today. With a clear focus on the future and the reality at hand, they steer their cultures forward in an ongoing and ultimately inspiring process.

"It's fascinating to watch," says Melvin Leong, Manager of Corporate and Marketing Communications at Changi Airport. "When people come to work here, whether in a restaurant, a retail location, an airline office or an immigration counter, first they go through the Changi Airport service training. Then, after they've worked here for a while, it's almost like a light bulb goes off. They see the reaction from travelers. They see other employees improving their service. And that's when it becomes real. That's when people begin to own it for themselves. Yes, we have people who are specifically responsible for our airport service initiatives. But, it doesn't take long before everyone realizes that they're driving these initiatives, too."

The airport builds an award-winning culture with a dynamic and frequently changing series of service classes, contests, recognition programs, communications, surveys, focus groups, and much more. You will learn how leading organizations drive their service cultures forward, and how you can achieve the same results or even better results where you work, in section 5 of the book, chapters 25 through 27.

How Does This Change Begin?

"OK, it's obvious that Changi Airport is a great example of surprising, personal, and stress-free service, and I can see that everyone plays a part," remarked Todd as he relaxed in one of the many massage chairs freely available throughout the airport. "But how do these things get started? What about the companies that have never really focused on service—much less an uplifting service culture? How does change start then? Can one person take the lead and change an existing culture?"

"Sure," I said. "This is just the gateway to Singapore. Now let me take you inside to a place where you might least expect to find an uplifting service culture, where people go when there is an accident, or a problem, or even after someone dies. I'll tell you the true story of how one man confronted the past and declared a cultural revolution and how every member of that organization made their service revolution come alive."

SECTION TWO

LEAD

CHAPTER 4

Taking the Lead

There was an ominous cloud hovering over Singapore. The air was wet and gray. As always, Mr. Lee awoke before sunrise. He drank his tea, ate his breakfast, and strapped on his sturdy work boots. Then, quietly, he snuck out of the house. This was his daily ritual for 13 years.

Mr. Lee worked on a loading dock in the shipyards. It was a physically taxing job, but well worth the exhaustion. The job provided enough money to give his wife and his two children a better life. And his shift, though long, ended before his children went to sleep. He could still see the two sons he loved while they did their homework in the evenings.

On this day in 1969, Mr. Lee's job was to help unload bags of rice from a ship arriving from Indonesia. Under normal circumstances, the job would take him and his team the entire day. But on this dark and rainy day, Mr. Lee never left work. He never finished unloading that ship. A misstep by a colleague toppled the cargo—burying Mr. Lee. The weight of the crash killed him instantly. And the accident left the Lee family emotionally and financially devastated.

In 1969, Singaporean workers like Mr. Lee found it impossible to buy insurance. His job was considered "high risk," and his wage wasn't enough to afford coverage. After the accident, his wife and children found themselves without a financial provider.

Family, friends, and neighbors offered as much as they could to help. In fact, the Ibrahim family—the Lees' next-door neighbors—offered as much support as they could afford. Mrs. Ibrahim cooked for the Lees. Mr. Ibrahim even offered the family a portion of his savings—but as a career bus driver, his finances barely paid his own family's bills.

Eventually, Mrs. Lee moved her sons to Malaysia where she accepted scattered jobs. The two boys, in their early and mid-teens, found trouble. One was jailed on drug charges. The other fled the area.

Ironically, if this had happened in 1970, just one year later, everything would have been different.

The new Singaporean government was beginning to transform the nation, and that meant vast social and economic changes. The government realized that many workers on the front lines of the country's industries couldn't find or afford insurance to protect themselves or their families. Yet accidents happen and unfortunate medical conditions do strike. If the nation's workers and their families were suffering from economic blows, the nation would suffer, too. This was unacceptable.

In 1970, Singapore's National Trades Union Congress (NTUC) set up an insurance cooperative with a mission and a social purpose unlike any other organization. The purpose of this new company, NTUC Income, was to provide affordable insurance products to the dockworkers, construction workers, and laborers like Mr. Lee who worked in high-risk, low-paying jobs. In fact, it was only a short time following Mr. Lee's accident when Mr. Ibrahim, the bus driver, purchased his insurance policy from NTUC Income with an affordable premium of $5.28 a month. The policy was in force for just three years when Mr. Ibrahim collapsed over his steering wheel one morning and died of a heart attack. His family—a wife and three children—were heartbroken over their loss, a caring husband and devoted father unexpectedly and suddenly gone.

But the insurance policy from NTUC Income paid them $5,500, enough money at the time to allow all three children to stay in school, grow up in the same neighborhood, and keep their friends. Eventually, all three children would attend college. One became an engineer. Another majored in business and finance. And the youngest became a teacher.

NTUC Income changed the lives and futures of numerous families by serving an underserved demographic, a population that other insurers refused to serve. NTUC Income became a trusted name in Singapore, a source of stability and a life saver for numerous families who, without it, would have suffered financial ruin.

Rising Expectations

Back in the 1970s, Singapore's government leaders envisioned creating a productivity-driven economy and culture. Agencies and organizations set up to protect the people's interests—such as NTUC Income—operated under policies that modeled the success of global manufacturing organizations and standards. They weren't thinking at the time about delivering world-class service as a national competitive advantage. They were focused on delivering risk-managed, low-priced, and zero-defect products and processes, and they succeeded within their own benchmarks.

Back when NTUC Income began, workers and their families became customers because they had no other choice. However, just because the company was created to serve a population that other insurers refused didn't mean it could thrive forever with an industrial model of service.

As the years passed, average household income grew from US$516 per person in 1965 to almost US$44,000 in 2010. NTUC Income realized it must compete with the more commercial insurance companies that were thriving in the new, increasingly affluent economy. Prospective customers had many choices. And they weren't choosing NTUC Income. The secure, stable, and reliable company had gained a reputation as "traditional and conservative." NTUC Income was not appealing for younger customers, and it was no longer attractive to those whose personal affluence had risen with the nation.

Enter Mr. Tan.

In 2007, the former CEO of NTUC Income retired after 30 years at the helm. He had built an institution that served the nation well. But a new CEO, Mr. Tan Suee Chieh, was hired to help uplift NTUC Income into the future. "Change was necessary," said Tan. "Income needed to be energized." The expectations placed on Tan's shoulders were hefty—raise the competitive standing of the cooperative to stand toe-to-toe with commercial insurance giants, while preserving and expanding the social purpose that made NTUC Income different from the beginning.

Made Different

"This is a cooperative?" asked Todd Nordstrom when I brought him to meet Mr. Tan. "The fun, bright orange branding messages remind me more of a fast-moving Internet company."

Todd was referring to massive orange decals facing the street communicating the "Made Different" slogan.

"Is this like a GEICO gecko advertising hook?" he asked.

"No." I chuckled. "This is more than a talking lizard—cute as it may be. This is energy. This is a mission. It's a game changer. And you'll soon see how seriously these folks take their brand. They live it."

Todd rolled his eyes at me as we walked to the elevators inside the building, but he smiled as he read the orange decals covering the elevator doors: a huge billboard communicating NTUC Income's service initiative "Service Alive!"

The doors opened. On the elevator stood two men and one woman. One of the men wore a bright orange tie. The other wore a crisp orange shirt. And the woman wore a bright orange bracelet wrapped around her wrist.

Todd smiled again. I couldn't wait to introduce him to Mr. Tan.

Declaring a New Beginning

How does an incoming leader transform a stable, conservative, and socially focused culture into an energetic, innovative, and commercially viable organization? Especially without offending or upsetting the people in the current customer base who have become used to, and appreciate, "the way things are."

Upon his appointment as CEO, Tan Suee Chieh dug deep into the founding principles of NTUC Income. He traced the organization's history, the original intentions of the founding fathers, and the vision of the nation's leaders who understood the importance of offering financial protection for those who worked day in and day out to secure Singapore's financial potential. He also dug in to the local perception of NTUC Income to find out exactly what potential customers would want from the company. How could they satisfy their social purpose, providing affordable insurance to low-wage workers, while still attracting profitable customers and competing with world-class competition?

The magnitude of this transition cannot be underestimated. It's not a simple case of adding customer service innovations. It's not like Domino's offering customers an online pizza tracker so they can follow their dinner from oven to doorstep. Or Home Depot ensuring that knowledgeable employees are roaming the aisles to help do-it-yourselfers. Or Carnival Cruise Lines adding rock-climbing walls and simulated surf pools to its well-appointed cruise ships. All of these examples are easy to spot; they are unique and intriguing.

NTUC Income faced a bigger challenge. It wasn't a failing company, but it was perceived to have become a boring company. It was achieving the goals originally established decades earlier, but this history would not ensure its vitality in the future. The company could do better, and be better.

Mr. Tan believed the company shouldn't be a fallback for the lower-income bracket. It should be a first choice for all income groups and a beacon of light offering transparency, trustworthiness, and uplifting service in an industry too often blamed for false promises, anxiety, and confusion. NTUC Income should reflect to its customers the safety and security of the nation. But it should also reveal the innovation, energy, and beauty that had become a part of Singapore's brand. And, it should surpass commercial competitors in the marketplace. Mr. Tan believed it should and could be absolutely world class, an icon of uplifting service, admired at home and abroad.

How does a company go from great to greater? How does one man generate an uplifting transformation after more than 40 years of standard practice? He makes a bold and very public declaration, which is exactly what Mr. Tan did on April 3, 2007, first at a company gathering with every member of the organization in attendance, and then the following day in a full-page advertisement in the local newspaper.

THE DECLARATION
at the Esplanade

Mr. Tan Suee Chieh, the new CEO of NTUC Income, held a town hall meeting with 1,600 of his staff and insurance advisers at the Esplanade on 3 April 2007. Below are excerpts of his speech which are relevant to all the stakeholders of NTUC Income.

Today marks a new beginning for NTUC Income. As we move forward, we must renew our commitments to our stakeholders and raise our own sights higher and further.

Let every customer know, that we will work always with your interests at heart. Every decision we take is calculated to protect your interests individually and as a whole. It is for you, that Income exists.

Let every competitor know, that with sweat, energy and determination we will compete with you on the platform of transparency, value for money and customer service, not for shareholder profits, but for the betterment of the people of Singapore.

Let every trade unionist know, that whilst we modernise Income and take it to greater heights, it is not a sign that we betray our roots, but we seek to perpetuate our relevance to serve both you and future generations of Singaporeans to come.

Let every partner know, whether you are an independent financial intermediary, a corporate agent, a car distributor, a motor workshop, a broker or a supplier, that we seek not to compete with you but to work with you, in a spirit of genuine partnership, to give our customers greater choice and better value.

Let our patron and supporter, the NTUC, and the people of Singapore know, that we are committed to our social cause. In line with the aspirations of the Labour Movement, we will be inclusive in our approach, so that we will serve wider segments of the Singaporean society, and that our actions and behaviours will bring you and the nation pride and joy.

To our insurance advisers, let me say this, we have a great opportunity, an opportunity, which we must grab with both our hands. With our strengths and our social purpose, your work is not just work. It is a cause; a cause to ensure every Singaporean is adequately protected against the uncertainties of life, and secured with a prosperous future, so that they can have the peace of mind to build Singapore today.

To our staff, let me say this. We have a great responsibility. A responsibility to do what is right for our customers, first time and every time. A responsibility which we all must welcome—because this is how we ensure our relevance, and more importantly, this is the right thing to do. And all of us have a great opportunity to grow with Income's success.

To our managers and the leaders in the company, let me say this. The time to exercise leadership is now. We have a lot to do and we must do them. Supported by a strong board with good minds and by a patron with the right heart, we can exercise our leadership confidently, secure with our belief that the pursuit of commercial excellence for a social purpose is unrivalled as the highest meaning in our professional lives.

My colleagues. We are a great co-operative, but the best is yet to come.

Declaring a Revolution

Mr. Tan's declaration attracted great interest, and a good dose of skepticism. The declaration was an affirmation, but it was unsettling, too. What would become of NTUC Income? What would it look, feel, and act like? And how would it perform?

"A transition like this is uncomfortable," said Mr. Tan. "We insure about 3.8 million people. Many of them were anxious. The company that was perceived as safe, because it didn't change, was now undergoing tremendous change."

"Umm, I'm guessing not everyone was happy," said Todd to Mr. Tan. "I mean, this was pretty dramatic. Did a lot of the employees and managers question your leadership? You walked in and turned everything orange."

Mr. Tan laughed. "It's change," he replied. "Change often creates dislike. There were, and I'm sure still are, people in this company who don't like the change."

Externally and internally, NTUC Income changed. Mr. Tan brought in a few new team members to work with him at the top. They changed the logo, the branding, and the advertising strategy. They added new innovative products and services, and reassessed what value meant in an industry marked by confusion. They recruited new people who shared their aggressive vision, and implemented new service education with every member of the team. And they transformed a weary culture into an engaged, enthusiastic, and energized team of professional people who understood and lived the company's purpose.

Oh, and amid the world's greatest economic recession since the company first opened its doors in 1970, while many famous firms in finance collapsed, NTUC Income became more successful and profitable than ever. For the first time, NTUC Income became the largest insurer in Singapore in life, motor, and health insurance. Number One.

How did Tan Suee Chieh lead this transformation?

Building a winning service culture isn't just about making declarations, or even about taking care of your customers. It is also about building the passion and practices for delivering great service inside and throughout the organization. True service leadership is not a demand for better performance pointed at the frontline service department. It's not a campaign slogan that gets splashed across the wall. True service leadership means creating an environment where every member of the team can lead—from the top down, from the bottom up, and from every position in the organization.

You read the declaration Mr. Tan gave publicly. Here now, is his bold internal declaration of a cultural revolution, shared with all staff members just four months later in another whole-company event.

OUR CULTURAL REVOLUTION

It is a revolution which calls for neither fear nor blood.

It calls for courage and for commitment.

It is not a revolution which pits one against another.

It unites our people to be the best people they can be.

It is a revolution to orchestrate independence of thought, and the courage to express it.

To establish that from now on, arguments will be won on the basis of merit, and not on position, status nor seniority.

Of challenging every past practice and accepting that a past practice may not be the best or even a necessary practice.

It is a revolution of the way we organize ourselves, talk to one another and of our willingness to take ownership.

It is a revolution of creating the spirit of innovation and creativity at all levels of the organization and not just the highest level.

It is a revolution of our own pace, speed and sense of urgency, and not waiting for directions from the top.

Of expressing our passion for excellence, and not of compliance and staying out of sight.

And that power will, from now on, belong to those who have the ideas and the drive to execute, and to those who have the vision and determination to take Income to the new world of a transformed Singapore.

It is a revolution of who we want to be and to make us proud to stand up for Income.

On how we want the rest of the world to see us and to know us, and that henceforth, the world will know Income will not accept second best.

It is a revolution of all our minds and all our hearts.

It is a revolution to transform NTUC Income.

It is a revolution to establish **The New Order of Things**.

Tan Suee Chieh
Chief Executive
NTUC Income

Leading from All Levels

Mr. Tan understood that service leadership had to start with him. He knew that he must be an example for employees at all levels of the company. But he also understood and deeply believed that eventually, everyone in the organization would need to become a leader of service if NTUC Income was truly to create an uplifting service culture.

Please take this point seriously. If your company is going to pursue building an uplifting service culture, leadership must initiate and support the process. But service leadership must be extended and ultimately embraced at all levels of the organization. Let's take a closer look at how to lead from all levels.

Top-Down Service Leadership

In this model, a service culture initiative gets a great start. The leader from the top becomes a role model for, and communicates with, everyone else in the organization. Mr. Tan did this consistently and effectively at NTUC Income.

However, this model alone is not enough because if even one manager in the middle doesn't set the right example or communicate the right service vision, a lot of employees are left behind. It's also not enough if anyone thinks that uplifting service or changing culture is a job for the people at the top. It's not. Uplifting service is everyone's job.

Bottom-Up Service Leadership

There are instances where frontline employees have initiated service revolutions—and have created award-winning service cultures. Consider the Pike Place Fish Market in Seattle, Washington. The company's leaders did not come to work one day and ask employees to throw and catch fish across the stall to give its customers an award-winning show. The employees came up with this idea themselves, and they enthusiastically put it into action.

But bottom-up service leadership typically doesn't happen, because frontline employees often aren't educated, enabled, or empowered to be proactive with new ideas for better service. Most simply follow procedure.

But a frontline employee can take the lead—with a customer to produce a better outcome, or with a colleague to create a better mood. A frontline supervisor can lead by encouraging, coaching, and training on the job. A manager can lead by reaching out to help colleagues in other departments, making service come alive inside the organization.

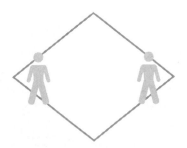

Leading from Every Position

Leading service from all levels means that every employee takes personal responsibility for providing better service in every situation his or her position empowers him or her to reach. Service leadership may be initiated from the top, but it is also embraced at the bottom and is encouraged and enabled everywhere in between. You don't need an important title to be a service leader. It's a responsibility you can choose for yourself.

When service leadership is alive at all levels in a large organization, frontline employees serve with passion because they understand the importance of their role, middle managers serve with passion because they understand the importance of their role, and senior leaders serve with passion because they understand the importance of their role. Indeed, it is everyone's role to take the lead in building a service culture.

Transformation Does Not Come Easily

"We had some struggles," admits Mr. Tan. "When we first started implementing our new service curriculum, we had some middle managers who wanted to bypass the classes everyone else was attending. Of course they are busy people. But it started to become a problem when they held people back from engaging in new service classes, or called them out of class to work on current projects. Or worse, they thought our revolutionary initiative was simply another customer service program for the frontline staff. That made me realize that I needed to prove the impact our new service curriculum could have on their people by showing them the impact on themselves. So we asked every middle manager to attend the classes themselves, and I joined each class they attended at the beginning, and the end. Then we launched a 'Show and Tell' service improvement contest requiring our managers to work closely with their staff to implement everything they learned. The result was tremendous."

Todd looked at me as we left the NTUC Income building that day. "That's an amazing story," he said. "A transformation like that isn't easy. Do you think most CEOs or executives hearing that story would believe they could accomplish the same degree of change, or the same results?"

"Only if they know, and follow," I replied, "the Seven Rules of Service Leadership."

CHAPTER 5

Leading from All Levels

It was 8 a.m. on Tuesday. Travis Hamilton, an independent film-maker from Arizona, arrived at a well-known local health spa with a truck full of video equipment. Piece by piece he hauled his equipment through the front doors, across the reception area, and up a long staircase to an outdoor balcony overlooking an attractive courtyard.

His job that day was to shoot a television commercial. Any video work he could get his hands on, like this commercial, was how Travis funded his dream of creating an independent feature film. However, while most commercial production companies would send a team of people to help set up and manage a video shoot like this, Travis did most of this work on his own.

Although he had heard stories about this spa's reputation for personal service and elegant surroundings, Travis had never shot video in a spa before. Soft lighting highlighted the beautiful décor, warm and welcoming treatment rooms, and a flower-filled courtyard. His job was to capture the experience this spa wanted to portray—impeccable service in a luxurious environment.

Travis lugged his equipment up the staircase to shoot the balcony, the first of many camera angles he would use in this commercial. When it was time for the next shot, he lugged his equipment back down the stairs for a series of close-ups, then outside for location shots, and later onto a rolling dolly for moving shots across the courtyard. And he did it all by himself.

Travis was extremely polite to everyone working at the spa. They were in the service business, and he wanted to fit in as a service professional. As he prepared each shot, he was careful that he was not rude in any way. He asked each employee for permission to set up the camera in his or her space. He asked the woman at the reception desk which outlets she preferred that he use to plug in his equipment. He asked the two actors if they were comfortable with each short scene before they moved on to the next. He made sure everyone was enjoying the experience.

Throughout the day, instead of telling people what to do, Travis asked. In fact, it seems the only thing Travis didn't ask for was help—except for one instance when he asked an older man quietly sweeping the floor if he would please hold that door open while Travis carried his equipment. The man agreed with a kind smile and then offered to help carry the equipment. Travis declined for the most part—except for a few larger items, for which he was most grateful. And, when the man handed him a cold bottle of water, Travis thanked him profusely.

At the end of the day, Travis took a deep breath and asked the receptionist if he could speak with the owner of the spa. He thought it was important to thank the person responsible for giving him this work. He understood that smaller, commercial jobs like this allowed him to pursue his dream.

Up the stairs, down the hall, and to the left was the spa owner's office. Inside was a large mahogany desk with a beautiful leather chair, and a polished table was nearby. Travis anxiously entered. He wasn't accustomed to dealing with seasoned business professionals. He wasn't accustomed to beautiful mahogany desks, leather chairs, and polished tables. And he surely wasn't expecting to find the same man who had swept the floors and held the door for him to be sitting behind that desk.

The owner of the spa was the person who served Travis the most that day. He smiled and welcomed Travis to come in and sit down for a moment to rest. Travis smiled back. The man kindly inquired what Travis would like to drink, and later thanked him for his service with a handwritten note and gift voucher, so he could enjoy a treatment at the spa.

"Now I get it," Travis thought. "No wonder this spa has such an outstanding reputation for service."

The Seven Rules of Service Leadership

Leaders can't just tell people how to serve; every day they must show people how to serve and teach them why it's so valuable. It would be easy to say that Mr. Tan of NTUC Income simply insisted on delivering better service or that the leadership team at Changi Airport issued a government order and demanded world-class service. But that's not how it works. People in every level of an organization will not engage in making a service vision come alive unless their leaders are living it, too.

In my experience working with leaders of many of the world's outstanding service organizations, I've discovered seven essential rules these leaders always follow. Some leverage the power of one rule more than another, and you may do the same. But each of these rules is essential to lead your team to success. In the chapters ahead you will find many examples, ideas, and suggestions for putting these rules to work.

Rule 1: Declare Service a Top Priority

NTUC Income is a clear example of how vital it is to declare service—and continuous service improvement—a top priority for the organization. The company was already a very large and successful organization when Mr. Tan was hired as CEO. But being large and commercially successful wasn't enough. Tan made clear public declarations that uplifting service was no longer just part of the business; it was now a top priority in his plans for cultural transformation. In fact, he willingly provoked the status quo by calling it a revolution.

Consider the companies you know well for their consistently high quality service, organizations that have built profitable and enduring reputations: Nordstrom, Disney, Southwest Airlines, Singapore Airlines, The Ritz-Carlton, and more recently Zappos. These companies consistently declare service a top priority and are vigorous in delivering what they declare.

Declaring service a top priority means senior leaders understand that focusing on service improvement leads to commercial results. Profit is the applause you receive for serving your customers well. When middle managers declare service a top priority, the message to everyone is clear: procedures and budgets surely count, but creating value for others counts the most. And when frontline employees declare service their top priority and delighting others becomes their goal, they uplift customer satisfaction—and job satisfaction, too.

You can declare service a top priority by putting it first on the agenda. You can declare service as a top priority to your customers and your colleagues in your speaking, writing, meetings, advertising, websites, newsletters, tweets, blog posts, updates, video clips, workshops, and daily actions.

Rule 2: Be a Great Role Model

Leaders are the people who others choose to follow, not those who simply tell other people what to do. By their own example, leaders inspire others to want to do what they do, too.

Let's consider just how large the impact of role modeling can be. A senior executive from Matsushita Electric (now operating as Panasonic Corporation) was visiting one of the company's manufacturing plants overseas. Because of his senior status within the organization, and because he had a legendary reputation for noticing small details, local employees cleaned up the plant and even rolled out a red carpet for his tour around the factory floor. Seven hundred workers in freshly cleaned uniforms stood shoulder to shoulder between the large machines. The executive, in a perfectly tailored pinstripe suit, walked slowly along the carpet, nodding with respect to the workers.

Then suddenly the executive turned, stepped off the soft red carpet, and walked slowly but deliberately toward one of the factory's largest machines. The executive's assistants whispered anxiously to each other. This detour was not on the schedule, and no one knew what to expect. Seven hundred workers watched him intently, wondering where he was going, and why?

He reached the large machine, paused, and took a deep breath. The eyes of the entire workforce were now glued to this storied executive from the head office. Seven hundred workers watched in amazement as he bent down, reached his hand just under the edge of the machine, and picked up a paperclip he had seen out of the corner of his eye. He stood up and tucked the paperclip into his suit pocket. He took another deep breath, turned, and quietly returned to the red carpet.

The room was silent.

There was no scolding. There wasn't a word said. But the message of this action resonated for years. The senior executive could have asked one of his entourage to fetch the paperclip. He could have told an employee to pick it up. He could have scolded, instructed, and sent out a memo, but he didn't. Instead, he simply modeled an expectation that everyone is responsible for maintaining the highest standards of cleanliness in the plant.

I learned of this incident from a man who was in the factory that day and saw this with his own eyes. He was moved with emotion as he told me the story more than 15 years later. "After that visit," he said, "our factory was the cleanest in the country. It wasn't because we bought more cleaning equipment or changed any of our housekeeping procedures. That one gesture made such a big impact that we held ourselves—and each other—to the same incredibly high standard."

Rule 3: Promote a Common Service Language

In military service, building and using a common language comes naturally. Leaders are promoted through the ranks and share a set of clear terms with their troops: "At ease," "Reporting for duty," "Attention!" But most of us don't serve in the military. In commercial and government organizations, language often evolves in functional silos, and in ways that don't connect.

People in the finance department think turning out reports faster equals better service. But their colleagues in other departments might actually prefer some help in reading those reports. Those in procurement think that getting a lower price is better service. But their colleagues may be seeking stronger partnerships with vendors. Human resources may assume more vacation time is better service for employees, when what employees really want is greater flexibility in health care and other benefits. Manufacturing believes delivering a defect-free product is its finest quality service. But the marketing and sales teams may prefer a wider range of newer products. Marketing thinks its service is better when the number of leads goes up. But sales may say just the opposite: they want fewer, but better-qualified, new leads. Finally, the sales team says its service should be measured by the number of new or increased sales. But what the company may need even more is consistent sales volume throughout the year.

Disconnects can also occur between levels of an organization. Managers talk about service metrics, benchmark scores, and growing share of wallet. Frontline workers talk about today's schedule, a colleague's problem, an angry customer's remark.

Everyone talks about better service from a perspective that makes perfect sense to him or her. What's missing is a common language to enable listening and understanding, clear distinctions to appreciate what other people want and value. To build a culture of uplifting service throughout an organization, leaders must promote a Common Service Language everyone can apply.

In section 4 of this book, you will discover and learn a new language that works beautifully for leaders and service providers in every function and position. "We need to polish those Perceptions Points before our service level drops below expected" (chapter 21). "Do we know which categories of The BIG Picture these new customers value most?" (chapter 22). "Let's close the loop on this Service Transaction, then explore for new opportunities to grow together" (chapter 26).

Asking your team to upgrade service without enabling language is unwise and inefficient. Giving them a Common Service Language but not using it yourself would be foolish. If you want everyone on your team to deliver uplifting service, you must speak fluently and frequently about it. This responsibility cannot be delegated away to the department of corporate communications. Nor can your use of service language be mere lip service only. You must demonstrate your understanding and commitment with observable and admirable actions. Using the words without the deeds has no more impact than idle chatter. "Walking the talk" and "talking the talk" go hand in hand. When service leaders speak and act, people listen and choose to follow.

Rule 4: Measure What Really Matters

Many people get confused when it comes to measuring service. This is understandable, because you can measure so many things: complaints, compliments, expectations, levels of engagement, relative importance, recent improvements, performance to standards, customer satisfaction, retention, intention to repurchase, referral, share of wallet, share of mind, and so much more. Once you count, track, interview, survey, focus group, or mystery shop, then you can deduce, derive, deep-dive, and try to decide what to do about it all. No wonder people get confused.

A service leader cuts through this confusion to measure what really matters. Start by recalling our definition: *Service is taking action to create value for someone else.* Then the two most important questions are these: Are your actions creating value? and, Are you taking enough new actions?

Some people will say this is far too simple, that many other measures must be taken into account. But let's explore this together, first from the top down, and then from the bottom up.

The ultimate objectives in business include top-line revenues, bottom-line profits, market share, reputation, shareholder value, and growth. These are all easily measured. But what happens before you can achieve your ultimate objectives? What is the leading indicator and reliable precursor to achieving those business objectives?

One way to predict higher share, reputation, and profits is to see if your index and survey scores are going up. When satisfaction scores, loyalty scores, share of wallet scores, and employee engagement scores are all improving, your ultimate objectives will improve, too.

What is a reliable precursor to index scores going up? One sure predictor of higher survey scores is a consistently higher volume of positive feedback. When kudos, compliments, and bouquets are coming to you in abundance, then your index scores and survey results will rise, too.

But what must happen before the compliments start pouring in? What is the essential precursor to getting positive feedback in the first place? Compliments happen when someone has an idea to serve someone else better and then takes action to make it real.

And what is the precursor of new ideas and actions? It's new thinking and new learning about customers, service, and value.

Now let's follow this same sequence from the bottom up. New learning about service leads to new ideas for giving better service to others, which leads to new action, which leads to more compliments, which leads to higher survey scores, which leads to more sales, referrals, loyalty, and profits.

Too many executives track the ultimate objectives from a distance and wonder how to get better results. Uplifting service leaders are closer to the action; they know the bull's-eye to hit and the needle to move are where people are working with customers and colleagues each day. They measure what really matters from the bottom up: new learning about service, new ideas to serve other people better, and new actions to create greater value.

How many new service ideas have you and your team created this week? How many new actions have you taken?

Rule 5: Empower Your Team

Empowerment is a buzzword in business, and many leaders and employees seem to fear it. What they really fear is someone who is empowered making a bad decision. If a leader is not confident in her people, she doesn't want to empower them with greater authority or a larger budget. And if an employee is not confident in his abilities and decisions, he often does not want the responsibility of being empowered.

In both cases, what's missing is not empowerment, but the coaching, mentoring, and encouraging that must go with it. If you knew your people would make good decisions, you would be glad to give them the authority to do so. And when your people feel confident they can make good decisions, they will be eager to have this freedom. Empowering others cannot and should not be decoupled from the responsibility to properly enable those you empower.

When Tan Suee Chieh at NTUC Income realized his middle managers weren't attending the new service courses and were not encouraging their team members to attend, he knew he could not force new ideas for better service on his people. He had to enable them and empower them to use those ideas and then appreciate the power of their actions. So he requested all middle managers to attend a full two-day service education course, and he personally opened each program by taking time to explain why he thought this was important. And then he came again to close each program, to listen to his managers and answer any questions.

Then he gave the managers an assignment they could only complete by engaging fully in the course content with the members of their own staff. He asked each manager to answer this question: "What changes will you make between May and October of this year that will put what you have learned into action?" That sounds like a simple assignment, but there was an enabling hook. The managers had to respond in a presentation with the members of their own teams, and they had to use the service language they just learned to explain their proposed new actions. Six months later, in October, each manager and his or her team presented again, now showcasing the results they had achieved. It's the combination that works: enabling with education and personal support and then empowering with a challenge to work together and achieve new results.

Rule 6: Remove the Roadblocks to Better Service

I recently stayed at a luxury resort in California, where I presented a keynote speech about Uplifting Service for an annual meeting of franchisees. The property was gorgeous. The rooms were spectacular. The people couldn't have been friendlier. And the food was sensational. But then one night, I invited some friends who lived in the area to join me for dinner at the resort. Our waiter explained that there was a special menu that night—spotlighting several of the chef's special dishes. We all looked at the menu to see if anything was appealing, and, after a few minutes, the waiter returned to take our orders.

"We'd like to order from the resort's standard dinner menu," I said. I had fallen in love with the salmon salad during my stay, and two of my guests were vegetarian—with nothing to choose from on the chef's menu.

"I'm sorry, we're only offering this menu tonight," said the waiter.

"Really?" I asked. "But I love that salmon salad, and two of my guests are vegetarian. I'm sure we could order these from your standard menu? Or from the room service menu?"

"Yes, sir," said the waiter, obviously uncomfortable. "If you go back to your room and order room service, then you can order the salmon salad or anything else on that menu."

"But isn't the food prepared in the same kitchen?" I asked.

"Yes, sir," replied the waiter. "But we're not allowed to serve anything in the restaurant tonight that's not on this special menu."

I understood the resort wanted to spotlight the chef's evening specialties. But the restaurant had created a major roadblock for the people who worked there, and it's not about the menu or the salmon salad. It's about the customer experience and the simple fact that the waiter wasn't given permission to serve. Imagine how thrilled and special we would have felt if he had said, "I'll make an exception for you tonight. And for your guests, I am sure we can come up with something deliciously special."

Most frontline staff members are taught to follow policies and procedures. Often they are hesitant to "break the rules." Yet some rules should be broken, changed, or at least seriously bent from time to time. What roadblocks to better service lurk inside your organization? What gets in your people's way? What slows them down? What prevents them from taking better care of your customers? What stops them from helping their colleagues? Service leaders ask these questions and remove the roadblocks they uncover.

Rule 7: Sustain Focus and Enthusiasm

It's not difficult to declare service as a top priority. What's challenging is keeping service top of mind when other issues clamor for attention. It's not hard to use a new language for better service; what's hard is using that language day after day until it becomes a habit. It may not be hard to track new service ideas and actions, but it can be difficult to keep them top of mind in the thinking of your team.

Sustaining focus and enthusiasm for service is vital when building an uplifting service culture, and world leaders seize every opportunity. When world-leading Singapore Airlines suffers business setbacks during events like the SARS outbreak, the attacks of 9-11, and dramatic financial crises, instead of laying off people in a knee-jerk reaction to cut costs, the company seizes the opportunity and brings its people in to attend new service enrichment courses. Think about that—when business returns to normal, Singapore Airlines employees are better trained and focused. They come out of each economic downturn even more committed to the company and to their customers: ready to serve with greater skills in languages, procedures, food, wine, and all kinds of special situations. No wonder it consistently leads the world in service.

Sustaining focus and enthusiasm is critical—in business, in life, and in service. This is not something leaders should view as a soft and therefore less important rule. Nor should it be entirely delegated to others. In fact, overlooking Rule 7 could be the mistake that derails all your plans and programs. How many diets fail because people can't sustain focus and enthusiasm? How many marriages fail for the same reasons? How many companies suffer from starting down a great path, but ultimately view the endeavor as a failure, simply because they couldn't sustain it?

There are many ways to sustain focus and enthusiasm for service, and the building blocks in the next section of this book will provide you with many examples. Or, you could share the stories you have already read with others where you work. What this book cannot provide is your sustained commitment to keep the focus and enthusiasm high, to put these ideas into action. That leadership must come from you.

Service Changes the World

"Everyone told me I had to try the chili crab," said Todd Nordstrom.

"I'll take you to East Coast Seafood across the street," I replied. "There are many seafood restaurants there, and they all serve chili crab, and a lot more."

He smiled. "I've heard it's the best in the world."

"Sure, but everyone who lives here in Singapore has a favorite restaurant for chili crab." I said. "People here can be very opinionated when it comes to food."

"So, which restaurant actually has the best?" he asked.

I laughed. "Todd, it's all fantastic. But I choose the place with the shortest line and the friendliest staff. If the service is slow, or the staff are not smiling, I move on to the next place."

"It's all about service with you, isn't it?" he asked.

"You better believe it," I said. "Now you're starting to see how I see the whole world. And you're seeing why I want to show you all these companies and introduce you to all these people. Now you're seeing why I do what I do."

Todd paused. He gazed out my living room window with his hands in his pockets. And, until he responded again, I had believed we were having a casual conversation.

"I get it," he said quietly.

"What do you mean?" I asked.

"Service changes the world," he said, still facing the window.

I paused and smiled. I was surprised, and delighted. Todd was beginning to understand.

"Come on." I said to my visitor and friend. "Let's go enjoy the best chili crab you'll ever eat."

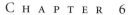

CHAPTER 6

The Journey to Magnificence

It was April of 2010. Eager crowds of people waited anxiously outside glass doorways—hoping to experience something magnificent. Inside, there were more than 4,000 team members in one of the biggest "pep rallies" of all time. This was not a high school pep rally. This one was for keeps. An unprecedented $5.7 billion had been invested, and the company's survival was hanging in the balance.

Tom Arasi stood on the other side of those glass doors. He watched the facial expressions. Tom felt the anticipation, and he took a deep breath.

"We knew we had built it," said Mr. Arasi. "And let me tell you, staring out into the sea of people, we expected challenges."

This is what happens when someone builds something great. There comes a time when all the vision, leadership, and effort align and combine into a single, unified structure. And that's when it takes on a life of its own.

Consider the Roman Coliseum. Think about the Eiffel Tower, the Sydney Opera House, the Golden Gate Bridge, or even Cinderella's Castle at Disneyland. All of these structures were built to serve a purpose. And, when they were finished, they became global icons.

Now consider the global icons of service. How were they built? What purpose did building a service culture serve? And at what point does an uplifting service culture take on a life of its own?

What does it take to build an icon? How do you create a miracle out of cement, glass, and steel? That was Tom Arasi's job as founding CEO of the Marina Bay Sands integrated resort, an enormous hotel, a convention center, a shopping mall, a museum, a theater, restaurants, and a casino all connected.

"There was a lot of pressure," said Mr. Arasi. "The process of building this place was intense. People who understand how aggressive this project was to undertake often ask if I would do it again—would I put myself and other people through that level of stress again?"

Mr. Arasi paused.

"I would," he said. "When I see what we created, and how much can be accomplished by getting people to see a shared vision, and how we felt when we realized that we had created something bigger than a really amazing building, yes, I'd do it all again. It's been a magnificent journey. And I would do it without pay. This property, and the human capital it took to deliver the performance, was nothing short of a once-in-a-lifetime phenomenon."

Let's backtrack to understand the aggressive process Mr. Arasi is referring to. In fact, just for a minute, consider the magnitude of activity required to build what is quickly becoming one of the world's most iconic pieces of architecture, a luxurious integrated resort that provides the stunning physical foundation for an emerging and iconic service culture.

To appreciate the achievement, it's crucial to understand that before Marina Bay Sands was built, gambling was illegal in Singapore, the landmass where it stands did not exist, and the world was in the midst of an economic catastrophe.

Yet, one of the most majestic and magnificent pieces of architecture known to humankind was built—for your pleasure, surprise, and delight.

Now, before you type "Marina Bay Sands" into a search engine to view a spectacular photograph of the building (which I do highly recommend), imagine one of the most unique examples of architecture in existence. First, the foundation of a massive multilevel convention center with over 1 million square feet of conference and exhibition space, an enormous shopping mall lined with 300 designer stores, more than 60 food and beverage outlets spread throughout the complex, with recreational amenities including two spectacular theaters, a world-class museum, an ice skating rink, and a casino.

Now, imagine three hourglass-shaped towers curving upward, each 57 stories tall, containing 2,600 hotel rooms, rising high above the foundation to overlook the ocean on one side and the city of Singapore on the other.

Incredible? This is only the beginning.

Now imagine those three tall towers connected at the top by an ocean liner looking structure that is host to a lush park including trees, flowers, and greenery 57 stories in the sky. High above the city, the 3,900-person-capacity Sands SkyPark is neighbor to restaurants, lounges, overlook posts, and an infinity swimming pool whose water meets the Singaporean sky.

Impressive design. Impressive construction. Impressive vision. And, impressive results. Marina Bay Sands is by far one of the most magnificent architectural, commercial, and cultural undertakings of our time—a completely integrated resort on one property and operated by one management team.

Still not enough for your imagination?

Then imagine this: it was built in just three years. And by the end of its first 12 months of operation, Marina Bay Sands had generated a staggering one billion dollars of EBITDA (earnings before interest, taxes, depreciation, and amortization). And the building hadn't even been finished.

Not Just a Pretty Face

Staring up at the three towers of Marina Bay Sands sent chills down the spines of Ryan Williams and his wife Sarah. Ryan had traveled to Singapore just once before. His first trip was business. This time, it was his honeymoon.

Williams had heard about Marina Bay Sands from a co-worker. He wanted his arrival with his bride to be perfect. He wanted her to be in awe. He wanted the next seven days of his life to be magical.

The unique architecture of Marina Bay Sands can impress just about anyone. And we already know that the new couple was excited. After all, they were on their honeymoon. They had landed and experienced the amazing interiors and friendly people at

Changi Airport. They hired a special taxi, and the driver had offered them a warm welcome and great service on the ride to Marina Bay Sands. But what happens to their once-in-a-lifetime experience if they don't receive magnificent service at one of the most magnificent resorts in the world?

Imagine how quickly the romance of the trip could be squashed if the check-in line at the resort took too long? Or, if the bellman wasn't friendly when delivering their bags? Or, if upon entering their room, they didn't find it impeccable, with every piece of furniture polished and every amenity in place?

Marina Bay Sands had a vision of becoming iconic to the world—in structure and in service. They were building the property during one of the worst economic downturns in history. They battled with deadlines and budgets and cleared construction and legal permit hurdles. And they were on a blazing path to hire enough new team members.

"We went from 100 to 6,500 team members in just 100 days," said Tom Arasi. "Every morning it was like walking into a new company—so many new faces."

This type of rapid hiring—especially recruiting department heads from all over the world—creates a new and even bigger challenge. How does an organization build an iconic service culture when new staff members are joining the company daily, by the hundreds?

Mr. Arasi couldn't just send out a memo that said, "Treat the customer well." He was in charge of one the world's newest and most carefully watched premier resorts—an integrated property where service standards and service experience needed to be the number one focus at every touchpoint. And it needed to be number one for customers from all over the world, served by brand-new team members from all over the world.

"We realized that we had built something magnificent," said Arasi. "But we also realized that we needed to focus just as much on building a service culture. And we needed to do it quickly. Not only was this a critical success factor for our operation. The entire country of Singapore needed us to deliver on the *magnificent* promise in support of the country's bold initiative to elevate its game on the world tourism scene."

Imagine the newlyweds, Mr. and Mrs. Williams, sitting down for a romantic dinner by candlelight in one of the many fine restaurants at Marina Bay Sands. The food is spectacular. The view is spectacular. The waiter goes out of his way to make recommendations for fine wines to pair with the couple's dinner selections. It's all perfect. Right?

"What time does the museum open in the morning?" asks Mr. Williams.

"And can you tell us how to get tickets for *The Lion King*?" asks Mrs. Williams.

"I'm sorry, I don't know anything about those things," replies the waiter. "I only work here in the restaurant."

Magnificent service? Well, it's not horrible for the waiter at a restaurant not to know the operating hours of a museum or the ticketing details for a famous show. But imagine how the evening would have been so much more delightful if the waiter had responded in a different manner.

Imagine the waiter says to Mr. Williams with a smile, "The museum is fabulous. And there is an amazing Salvador Dalí exhibit on display there right now. It opens at 10:00 in the morning and stays open until 10:00 every night, even on holidays.

"And tickets for *The Lion King*? I saw it myself. It's great!" he says turning to Mrs. Williams. "The show starts at 8:00 every night except Monday, and on weekends there is a matinee at 2:00. I can contact the concierge if you would like tickets."

Now think about what those two simple statements require: a common service vision that spans the property, the wide range of product knowledge a waiter must learn and master, and the active cooperation of people and systems across so many departments.

"Just because you hire the right people, build an incredible resort, and offer the world the finest activities and amenities, doesn't mean you've created the ultimate experience," said Arasi. "If we didn't build a solid service culture, the whole thing could come crashing down on us. And I'll be blunt. Those first frenetic and tense days that we were open, we learned very quickly the importance of getting our cultural building blocks in place."

One early example of how much Marina Bay Sands needed to implement the building blocks of a common and uplifting service culture was during the property's grand opening of the world-famous play *The Lion King* in the theaters at Marina Bay Sands. *The Lion King* was a natural choice for the opening show in "The Lion City" of Singapore. It was promoted heavily in the city and throughout the region. Marina Bay Sands expected—and enjoyed—a massive response.

But here's the rub. To the hotel guests on opening night, to those customers who traveled across the globe to experience the magnificence of Marina Bay Sands, the stage was completely dark. Throughout all the promotion, the marketing, and the dollars invested in advertising the opening night, Marina Bay Sands forgot to inform their own in-house guests. The first audience to see *The Lion King* included just four guests of the resort.

What would your perception of service be if you flew into Singapore, stayed at Marina Bay Sands, and read in the paper the following day that you could have seen the opening night of *The Lion King* in your resort?

"We built the property quickly," said George Tanasijevich, the President and CEO who followed Tom Arasi's almost two-year tenure. "Tom Arasi got Marina Bay Sands built and took us through our first difficult year of operation. Now we need to build a world-class service culture even faster."

The Architecture to Build an Uplifting Service Culture

Over the past 25 years I've studied countless companies and seen their service philosophies in action. I've interviewed thousands of team members and their leaders. I am deeply inquisitive when exploring how people's attitudes, policies, and practices evolve in an organization, and seeing how it all comes together when building an uplifting service culture.

I have witnessed winning service cultures rise to great heights. I have seen service cultures form in different industries and countries all over the world. Some have been driven by their struggle to compete, to overcome difficulties, or to solve a persistent problem.

Some were motivated by ambitious goals to achieve, mergers to complete, or new markets to penetrate and conquer. And some were simply inspired by people who saw the world through a wider lens—who believed in creating an uplifting service culture as a purpose greater than themselves.

There is an amazing constant among the successful companies and organizations I have encountered. A clear architecture for engineering a powerful service culture emerges over and over again. This common architecture involves many areas and activities that major organizations already use. They require thoughtful planning, coordinated activity, and lead to rewarding results.

Even more intriguing, I could see which elements were missing, or out of alignment, each time I encountered an organization with a struggling or failing service culture. And the reason was also clear: while these areas may all be active inside an organization, they are often managed by different departments and are not planned, deployed, or integrated with a unifying purpose or vision. This leads to disjointed and disconnected efforts and to confusing and even contradictory messages to team members.

At the top of this proven architecture is Service Leadership, which we have explored in this section. Actionable Service Education forms a vital foundation for continuous learning and service improvement. You will discover the fundamental service principles of uplifting service—and how to apply them in every job, role, and situation—in section 4, Learn.

Connecting service leadership with service education is a set of important and interconnected areas I call "The 12 Building Blocks of Service Culture." In the following chapters, we'll explore each of these essential building blocks in detail:

1. Common Service Language

Widely understood and frequently used by service providers throughout the organization, a Common Service Language enables clear communication and supports the delivery of superior internal and external service.

2. Engaging Service Vision

Eagerly embraced and supported, an Engaging Service Vision energizes everyone. Each person sees how the vision applies to his or her work and takes action to make the vision real.

3. Service Recruitment

Effective Service Recruitment attracts people who support your service vision and keeps out those who may be technically qualified but not aligned with your vision, spirit, and values.

4. Service Orientation

Service Orientation for your new staff members must be welcoming and realistic. New team members should feel informed, inspired, and encouraged to contribute to your culture.

5. Service Communications

Vibrant Service Communications inform and educate. Creative communication channels reach everyone with relevant information, timely customer feedback, uplifting service stories, and current challenges and objectives.

6. Service Recognition and Rewards

Service Recognition and Rewards motivate your team to celebrate service improvements and achievements. Acknowledgment, incentives, prizes, promotions, and praise—all help to focus attention and to encourage greater results.

7. Voice of the Customer

Voice of the Customer activities capture your customers' comments, compliments, and complaints. These vital voices must be shared with service providers throughout your organization.

8. Service Measures and Metrics

Measure what matters to focus attention, design new action, and create positive service results. Your people must understand what is being measured, and why, and what must be done to hit the bull's-eye.

9. Service Improvement Process

A strong Service Improvement Process ensures that continuous service improvement is everyone's ongoing project. Keep your methods vibrant and varied; keep participation levels high.

10. Service Recovery and Guarantees

When things go wrong, bounce back! Effective Service Recovery and Guarantees turn upset customers into loyal advocates and team members into true believers.

11. Service Benchmarking

Discover and apply best practices from other organizations inside and outside your industry. Service Benchmarking reveals what others do to improve service and points to new ways you can upgrade yours.

12. Service Role Models

Everyone is a Service Role Model. Everyone is watching. Leaders, managers, and frontline staff must walk-the-talk with powerful personal actions every day.

While you will see a method to the order in which I present and explain these building blocks, you may employ them in a different order in your organization. You may choose to focus first on any building block for which there is a current need or challenge in your organization. You may choose to start where there is low-hanging fruit, with fast results available from relatively little effort. You may choose to tackle a difficult or complicated area sometime later. Or you might work on an area in which the need is great or the impact will be most apparent.

Two things are certain from all my years of study and in all the organizations I have had the privilege to help. First, these 12 areas are often seen as the responsibility of management, but everyone at every level can contribute with his or her ideas and actions. Second, when these building blocks are connected, when they are aligned to support each other, you will enjoy powerful synergies that are currently untapped and experience a dramatic acceleration in performance.

Successful Architecture Is the Key

"Is that a flower?" asked Todd. He was standing on the 57th floor of the SkyPark and pointing at a white floral-structured building far below the towers of Marina Bay Sands. "That building is shaped just like a flower."

I explained that he was seeing the new ArtScience Museum from above, its petals pointing toward the sky, an open blossom inviting the people and the prosperity of the world to come enjoy a visit.

"Now look over there," I said, pointing in the opposite direction. "They're constructing a whole garden of buildings; it's called

Gardens by the Bay. It's an immense botanical garden filled with elegant shops and world-class restaurants.

"And look there," I said one more time, pointing in a third direction. A huge wheel with large pods each holding up to 30 people arced high over the ground. The Singapore Flyer was offering another wide and clear view of the harbor and the city.

"This is amazing," Todd responded. "It's hard to believe these are buildings. How do they build those? It almost seems impossible."

His question was ironic given the perch from which he stood, 57 stories in the air next to an enormous swimming pool that curved through the clouds.

"It's all in the architecture," I said. "Anything is possible with the right architecture. You can build amazing buildings, and you can build cultures of service that are equally amazing."

SECTION THREE

BUILD

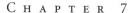

CHAPTER 7

Common Service Language

Using and promoting a Common Service Language is the first building block in your uplifting service culture. Why does this building block come first? Because human beings create the world in which we live by using language. We create meaning with language, and we can change our world by inventing or adopting new language.

Here's an example. Singapore is a fascinating mix of races, religions, and cultures with four official languages: English, Malay, Mandarin, and Tamil. A friendly common language, "Singlish," informally unites the country. Speakers are famous for putting "lah" after certain words like "OK-lah" and for short, punchy phrases such as: "So how?" "Can or cannot?" and "Why you so like dat?" Singlish is concise and efficient. Its speakers are focused on achieving the goal of any interaction. And it works. But it is not endorsed by the elected leaders of the country. Instead, the government conducts "Speak Good English" and "Speak Proper Mandarin" campaigns to encourage a more fluent and globally competitive workforce.

Singapore's leaders may not encourage Singlish, but they do understand the power of a Common Service Language when it comes to building service culture. Consider the problem faced by the Singapore Public Service—a wide-ranging system of government with 127,000 officers in 15 ministries and more than 50 statutory boards. Imagine a citizen, a tourist, or an employer with a question, trying to figure out which office to call? All too often, callers would make an attempt, only to hear a public servant say, "Sorry, you've called the wrong office." That's not world-class service.

So Singapore's Public Service leaders created a new phrase—and a philosophy—by implementing a policy called "No Wrong Door." Today, if you call the wrong government office, a public servant will take personal responsibility to transfer you to the right officer in another government agency, and he or she won't let you go until you have been successfully connected. "No Wrong Door" highlights the power of a Common Service Language: it's simple, memorable, and effective.

Singapore Airlines is widely recognized for consistently impeccable service standards. The company is also a world-class case study in the development and use of Common Service Language. In the 1970s, the airline adopted service as its core differentiating strategy with the aspiring tagline, "Service Even Other Airlines Talk About," and created the popular Singapore Girl icon as the in-flight personification of this promise. In 1987, the company wanted to raise service standards on the ground to match their well-deserved reputation in the air. A new phrase and educational program was created called "Outstanding Service on the Ground" (OSG). All over the world, Singapore Airlines employees learned the meaning of this acronym and how to put it into action. Although the program was phased out a decade later, the common language persists in telex messages like this: "PLS DAPO OSG PAX @ LAX." Translation: "Please do all possible to provide outstanding service on the ground for this passenger on arrival at Los Angeles International Airport." In the late 1990s, a program to succeed OSG was created called "Transforming Customer Service" (TCS). And in 2003 a new program for cabin crew was launched highlighting the company's defining aspiration to provide service that far exceeds the competition: "Service Over and Above the Rest" (SOAR).

Consider also how Microsoft added a Common Service Language to help create more desirable resolutions for its customers. For many years Microsoft has tracked "first contact resolution," a measure of how quickly it resolves an issue the first time a customer or partner makes contact. First contact resolution metrics are common throughout this satisfaction-driven software company. Dashboards show in numbers and percentages how many problems are resolved in less than 8 hours, between 8 and 24 hours, longer than 24 hours, or not resolved at all. When Microsoft learned the language of uplifting service, it added a new column called "Service Classification." Now, alongside the impersonal statistics is a rating of the customer's experience using some of the terms you will learn in section 4 of this book: *criminal, basic, expected,* and *desired.*

With the addition of this new service language, managers are asking new and sometimes unsettling questions. Instead of purely task and technical queries such as, "How can we reduce this number by 10 percent to hit our quarterly target?" they are now asking questions about the customer and partner experience: "This dashboard says that only 66 percent of our customers are getting what they desire. Then what is everyone else getting? And what are we doing about it?"

What's Your Common Service Language?

Your Common Service Language may become as famous as Disney referring to its employees as cast members or Subway calling its employees sandwich artists. Your language may become so strong that it permeates the organization and even society at large. Before Starbucks became popular, the most common phrase associated with coffee in America was the "bottomless cup." Today, all over the country and the world, customers order grande, non-fat cappuccinos, with extra shots, and dry.

Many organizations don't realize they already have a Common Service Language—and in some unfortunate cases it's not positive at all. The manager at a radio station I consulted with once joked, "When listeners complain, we instruct our people to say, 'When the bill arrives for your listening pleasure, just don't pay it.'" That's terrible language for a leader to employ or to ask his or her employees to use.

To build an uplifting service culture, your Common Service Language is a critical building block to clarify meaning, to promote purpose, and to align everyone's intentions and objectives. It should be easy to understand and easy to apply in real service situations. It must make sense for internal and external service providers and for team members at every level of the organization. Your Common Service Language should be meaningful and attractive—a shared vocabulary to focus the attention and the actions of your team.

Parkway Health has developed its Common Service Language much further along the proven path. They have created five core service values, each one connected to the word UP, reflecting its intention and aspiration to be distinguished in the medical field by its uplifting service culture. The articulation of these five values includes language that is appealing to the head, guiding to the hands, and uplifting for the hearts of nurses, doctors, lab technicians, orderlies, and every Parkway Health team member. This is Common Service Language hard at work, reminding everyone each day what to know, what to say, and what to do.

Naiade Resorts was the name of one the largest hotel groups in Mauritius, with nine resorts on the islands of Mauritius, Reunion, and Maldives. It recently completed a dramatic transformation to a new brand and style of service called "Island Light." Its vision is "Each Moment Matters" in fulfilling its uplifting purpose of "Helping People Celebrate Life." The brand transformation from Naiade to LUX* Island Resorts was an extraordinary project involving new images and artwork and 50 creative scenes, including secret snack bars, spontaneous ice cream stands, and free phone calls

STAND UP

I pledge that I CAN (and I WILL) **take personal responsibility** to provide superior service to all my internal partners and external customers

SUIT UP

I will pay special attention to my **personal grooming, dress code, verbal, and written communications**

SPEAK UP

I will create a **positive first** and **last impression** by always being the first to extend a **greeting, smile** and **a word of thanks** (where appropriate)

STEP UP

I will seek to understand the **service value** of the people whom I serve and will strive to **exceed** their expectation on all occasions

STAY UP

I will seek to deliver service **consistently** at the **desired** level and look for opportunities to be **surprising** and **unbelievable** home for guests. Transforming the attitude and behavior of more than 2,500 employees was equally ambitious and required its own special image and a new language. While a beautiful butterfly captures the color and elegance of the new LUX* brand, the remarkable transformation from a caterpillar to the butterfly characterizes the challenges for each resort team member. Paul Jones, CEO of LUX* Island Resorts, is fond of posing this question to his team: "As you serve our guests and each other today, are you a caterpillar or a butterfly?"

Questions for Service Providers

- Do you know the Common Service Language in your organization? If you don't yet have such a language, can you help create one?
- Do you use a Common Service Language every day? How can you use this language more frequently or creatively to make your service culture stronger?

Questions for Service Leaders

- Have you developed a constructive and effective Common Service Language? If you have not yet done this, who will help you create it?
- Do you actively use and promote a positive Common Service Language? Do you "talk the talk" so your team can hear you use it every day?
- Have you embedded a Common Service Language into your systems and procedures? Does working in your organization naturally guide your team to hear, read, and use it?

CHAPTER 8

Engaging Service Vision

In 1985 an advertising campaign changed the state of Texas forever.

Imagine you live in the largest state in the continental United States. You're on a road trip with your family, gazing out at seemingly endless stretches of highway. In the distance you may see rolling hills, parched deserts, massive ranches, major rivers, or gorgeous city skylines.

If you were traveling these highways in the early 1980s, you would also notice something much less pleasant—a lot of garbage, trash and litter along the road. Littering had become a monstrous problem. The Texas Department of Transportation knew the problem needed to be addressed. The state budget for roadside cleanup was growing as fast as the piles of litter.

Texans are proud of their heritage. Many grew up at rodeos, working at cattle ranches and oil refineries. They are the real cowboys in the United States. And, if you want them to stop throwing trash out of their pickup truck windows, a public service announcement that says "Keep Texas Beautiful" just isn't going to work.

But what about a campaign that reaches deep into the psyche of the rough-and-tumble Texas crowd, drawing on their toughness, their pride, and their very identity as Texans? The new campaign was a bold, confident, and very public challenge: "Don't Mess with Texas."

Widely embraced since its debut, "Don't Mess with Texas" became an engaging vision for the State of Texas and is credited for reducing roadside litter by 72 percent in just the first four years. The message lives on today as a battle cry for Texas pride that is recognized around the world.

That's what Engaging Service Visions do—they unify and energize everyone in an organization. They pose a possibility each person can understand and aim to achieve in his or her work, role, team, and organization. An Engaging Service Vision guides everyone toward action to make the vision real. It doesn't matter whether you call this building block your service vision, mission, core value, guiding principle, credo, motto, slogan, saying, or tagline. What matters is that your Engaging Service Vision is *engaging*.

When I started working with Nokia Siemens Networks, the executive board had recently approved a new marketing position: "Knowing How." This promoted Nokia Siemens Networks' well-known and widely respected strengths for technical expertise. But the company was being challenged by Chinese competitors that didn't necessarily know more, but were doing more for customers with large teams of lower-paid workers.

"Knowing How" is important, but what really matters is doing something with your knowledge to help someone else. The company's global service leadership team convened in India under the guidance of Mr. Rajeev Suri, who would soon become CEO of the entire organization. "Knowing How" evolved to "Knowing How, Doing Now," which was better, but still left something missing. What is the purpose of doing now? What is the intended result?

The air in the room was thick with focus and the frustration that often accompanies a vision-crafting effort. One of the leaders chuckled quietly and then smiled. Not known for hyperbole or exaggeration, he expressed solid confidence in the company when he said, "Know How, Act Now, Create Wow!"

This simple but powerful phrase has become a guiding focus for more than 60,000 Nokia Siemens Networks employees worldwide. "Know How" means know your customers, what they want, what they need, what you can do to help, and what your competitors are doing differently or better than you. "Act Now" means don't wait, reach out, take action, and make things happen. "Create Wow" means surprise customers, delight colleagues, go beyond expectations, and create wow—right now.

Consider NTUC Income, in early stages of its cultural revolution, working hard to overcome years of civil service–styled mission, vision, and values statements. Members of the Executive Committee showed me a long list of proposed service standards that read more like a compliance manual than a guideline for delighting anyone. I read the list in their boardroom and sighed. "These statements feel so dead. You really need something more alive."

The CEO heard what he had been listening for and jumped. "That's it! When our team members come to work, we want them to feel alive. When we serve our customers at the counter and over the phone, we want them to feel alive. When our agents serve customers in the field, we want them both to feel alive. That's our vision for the new style of NTUC Income's service: 'Service Alive!'"

Imagine going to work with the intention that every contact you have with someone else will leave him or her feeling more alive. So simple, so powerful, and so effective. Today, NTUC Income uses "Service Alive!" as an umbrella theme for many of its programs of service recruitment, orientation, communication, recognition, continuous improvement, and sales support.

An Engaging Service Vision is like a mantra to motivate your team and keep them focused on uplifting service. Sometimes the mantra will evolve. Marina Bay Sands opened its doors with a powerful internal statement to boost employee morale to the same soaring heights as the resort's stunning 57th story SkyPark: "We are Magnificent!"

This engaging vision kept morale running high through the early challenges facing any new resort, especially one with such a high profile, complexity, and size. But as the team members adjusted to daily challenges, they also understood that being magnificent is not just a moment in time. It is an endless quest to deliver the experience of magnificence to every visitor and to every team member as well. The point is not to be magnificent, but to make sure that the *experience* of magnificence is enjoyed by others.

As Marina Bay Sands evolved, its vision evolved from "We are Magnificent" to "The Journey to Magnificence." This Engaging Service Vision lives today in the actions of every team member and in the many uplifting service experiences they create.

These simple phrases may seem like just a nice collection of words. But the power of these words should not be underestimated. Companies that take the time to define, refine, and craft an Engaging Service Vision arrive at a greater understanding of their value, their customers, and themselves.

Engaging Your Employees

Employees are the people who make a service vision come alive. They make it real with the actions they take every day. For these vital service providers, an Engaging Service Vision activates creativity, motivates new action, and inspires them to deliver uplifting service experiences every day.

The courier company TNT uses a simple yet effective vision in Asia: "We put the *WOW* in service!" For their truck drivers, package sorters, and call-center employees, this simplicity and excitement works.

I called TNT to schedule a package pickup one rainy afternoon. After the service representative confirmed my address, package contents, weight, and final destination, she asked if she could tell me one more thing, and I replied "Of course."

Her tone changed slightly, and she spoke a bit more slowly than before. "Mr. Kaufman," she said. "It's raining here, but that's OK. Because customers like you put the sunshine in our lives."

I smiled and laughed. What she said wasn't in any script. It wasn't the company standard. It was an uplifting action from a tuned-in team member with an Engaging Service Vision. She made it come alive on a dreary afternoon. She put the *WOW* in service.

Engaging Your Customers

Your Engaging Service Vision can also resonate with the customers you serve. At Southwest Airlines, the Engaging Service Vision is "We make flying fun." That's why their cabin crew dress up in costumes on Halloween, why they sing "Happy Birthday" to passengers on the plane, and why a top ranked video for Southwest Airlines on YouTube is an upbeat member of its cabin crew rapping the preflight announcements (check it out).

This Engaging Service Vision is why Southwest Airlines won't hire new staff without a sense of humor, why the staff ask passengers to say hello to strangers across the aisle, and why they make announcements like this one before takeoff: "Ladies and Gentlemen, in the unlikely event of loss of cabin pressure, the oxygen mask will fall from the ceiling above you. If you are traveling with a child, please put the mask on yourself first, and then assist your child. If you are traveling with more than one child, please decide now which one you love more." It's not just the passengers with children who laugh. Everyone cracks a smile, everyone knows it's just for fun, and everyone is engaged.

Engaging Your Partners

Changi Airport has 28,000 employees who come to work every day for 219 different organizations: airlines, police, customs, immigration, restaurants, retail outlets, and banks. Imagine the fragmentation and confusion that could occur if everyone did not understand and share the same vision.

When you are in an unfamiliar airport and you have a question, whom will you ask? Will you pause to locate the official Information Counter and then walk over to patiently wait for your turn? Or will you ask just about anyone you see wearing any kind of uniform or working in any outlet, anyone who works inside the building?

At Changi Airport, people who work in the coffee shops know the departure gate locations and the fastest ways to get there. Airline employees who work at the gates know where you can buy last-minute souvenirs. Airport police can tell you how to find the post office and what time it opens. Immigration and Customs officers will gladly answer your questions about how to get into town.

How do the airport authorities create this community passionately dedicated to service, assistance, and information? They start with an Engaging Service Vision, "Many Partners, Many Missions, One Changi." At this remarkable gateway, everyone works together to create positive experiences every day.

What's Your Engaging Service Vision?

An Engaging Service Vision can differentiate you from everyone else, communicating your advantage as an upbeat employer, your reputation as an uplifting service provider, and your value as a vibrant community member.

When you compete on lower prices, then anyone cheaper can beat you. When you compete with a newer product, anyone's newer product will grab the spotlight. But when you compete with an Engaging Service Vision that shapes the entire culture, then you compete on the quality of relationships you build and the experiences you provide. You stand out for your commitment to new action creating greater value for others. When you compete on uplifting service, you compete with a vision to win. It's extremely difficult for your competitors to challenge and beat your organization when your service performance is continuously improving.

An Engaging Service Vision should be inspiring, motivating, guiding, and uplifting for your service providers and for your customers. Is yours?

Questions for Service Providers

- Do you know your organization's Engaging Service Vision? Can you share what it means in your own words?
- What actions can you take today to make your service vision come alive for your customers and your colleagues?

Questions for Service Leaders

- Do you have an Engaging Service Vision that stimulates the creativity and activates the service passion in your team?
- Are you enthusiastically sharing examples of your service vision in action with your employees, customers, and partners?
- How can you link your Service Vision to other culture building blocks: Service Recruitment, Service Orientation, Service Communications, and Service Recognition and Rewards?

CHAPTER 9

Service Recruitment

It's estimated that Google receives more than half a million resumes each year. It's no secret that the company is one of today's most sought after employers and most enviable work environments. Google wants to hire the best employees in the world. To help Google choose the right candidate, the company has developed an interview process that is widely recognized as one of the most rigorous employment screenings in the world.

Imagine you choose to apply. First, your resume is reviewed by the recruiting department. Keep in mind the vast majority are screened out on first pass. Second, if your resume survives the initial reviews, you will be contacted for a 30 to 40 minute telephone interview. If you make it past the telephone interview you will be invited to the Google office for onsite interviews with team members and managers of the department you are seeking to join. You will be carefully assessed for appropriate knowledge, innovative thinking, problem solving skills, and technical abilities.

Finally, if you are still in the running, you will be asked to return again for another round of interviews. You will meet with at least four different members of the Google team, including managers and potential colleagues, to see if you're the right cultural fit—to assess if you are sufficiently "Googley." Google believes that great people are attracted by, and attracted to, other great people. So, by involving so many people in the hiring process, Google is more likely to find, select, and invite employees who will thrive and stay at Google.

Google is a unique kind of service organization, dedicated to delivering all the information in the world in the best, fastest, and most accessible manner. Google's first core principle is "Focus on the user and all else will follow." Everything they do is to provide the best possible user experience.

But very few of the company's employees personally interact with customers. Imagine a brilliant programmer who sits behind a screen all day writing unbeatable code or inventing the next world-changing algorithm. Maybe he or she never has to crack a smile, shake a hand, or meet a user or an advertiser face-to-face. But this employee does need to work smoothly with his or her colleagues. That's why Google puts such a premium on recruiting and hiring only those who fit with the company's brilliant and "Googley" culture. Getting the right people on the bus is especially important when you are driving an extraordinary bus.

Zappos is as exceptional as Google, but has a completely different company culture. The online shopping company is widely recognized for providing intensely personal service and for cultivating a wacky service culture. The company's ten core values include not only "Deliver WOW Through Service," which is not unusual, but also "Create Fun and a Little Weirdness."

To make sure new hires fit into their curious culture, Zappos asks job seekers to be a little weird in their job application. Read this copy from the jobs page of the Zappos website; it's easy to see how its recruitment strategy is reinforcing the service culture.

JOBS.ZAPPOS.COM

The Zappos Family currently has career opportunities in 2 fabulous locations. One location is in the "City of Sin." Yep, Las Vegas, Nevada. Our other location is home to the Jim Beam Distillery and the Zappos Fulfillment Centers. You got it, Shepherdsville, Kentucky. We do not currently have any work from home opportunities. (Sorry!)

Please check out the Zappos Family's 10 Core Values before applying! They are the heart and soul of our culture and central to how we do business. If you are "fun and a little weird"—and think the other 9 Core Values fit you, too— please take a look at our openings, find the one or two that best fit your skills, experience and interest!

Why consider opportunities with us? In January 2011, Zappos.com, Inc. and its affiliates were named #6 on the 2011 Fortune: 100 Best Companies to Work For List.

And. . . we're hiring like crazy right now, and looking for smart, forward-thinking problem solvers to join our world-class, and fairly wacky team.

PS: At the Zappos Family of Companies, over-sized egos are not welcome. Over-sized Eggos, however, are most welcome and appreciated!

Oh, and one more thing! Cover letters are sooooo old-fashioned, don't you think? Show us who you are with a cover letter VIDEO! You will be able to upload one when applying for a position.

Google, Zappos, and many other service leaders know it is much easier to build a strong culture by hiring new people with the right attitude than to hire people for their skills alone and then try to align them around a common service vision. That's why Service Recruitment is such an important building block of service culture. Each new hire either makes your culture stronger or makes your challenge to build a great service culture a little harder. The right people pull naturally in the right direction. While cultural misfits may be incredibly talented, well-connected, or experienced in a specific area, their impact on the team can be confusing or downright disruptive. Every new hire sends a message to everyone else. Either you are committed to your service culture and hire good people to prove it, or your commitment is shallow lip service only, and your next hire also proves it.

How to Attract and Recruit the Right Service Talent

There is a time-tested maxim: what you think about expands in life, and what you focus on becomes clearer. What you see and say repeatedly will shape the way you live today and who you will become tomorrow.

You can apply this principle when recruiting new team members by following these five steps to hire the right talent for your service culture. Start by making it easy for candidates to consistently see, hear, and understand what your organization thinks about service. Those who align with your vision and values will be drawn closer and want to learn more about your spirit and purpose. Those who think, feel, or believe differently won't be attracted, and will naturally select themselves out. Both are positive outcomes for your culture and your future.

1. Share Your Engaging Service Vision

Use every opportunity to explain your Engaging Service Vision to prospective candidates. Place an uplifting message about your company culture on the website, in your employment ads, and in all the literature. Stress the importance of your service vision with your staff when you ask them to make new employee referrals and recommendations.

When job seekers apply, ask them to share in their own words what your service vision means to them. You can quickly check if candidates are aligned with your service vision by asking good questions and listening carefully to their answers.

For example, if your vision includes being proactive in adding value, you might ask, "What do you consider great service when helping new customers?" If an applicant says, "Giving them exactly what they ask for and doing it quickly," that's different from a candidate who says, "Giving new customers what they ask for, but also making recommendations to help them understand what might help them even more." If your vision includes going the extra mile, you might ask, "Tell me about a time you were most proud of your service achievement." If an applicant proudly explains how he or she delivered a project on time and on budget, that's different from someone who tells you about things he or she did for someone else that were never planned for in the first place. If your vision involves working closely as a collaborating team, you could ask, "Tell me how you achieved one of your greatest service successes." If the candidate responds with lots of "I," "my," and "me," that's different from someone who tells you about "us," "our," and "we."

2. Involve Your Culture Leaders

As the service culture in your organization grows stronger, some of your team members will become culture leaders. These people are like tuning forks—vibrating strongly, keeping everyone else in key, and helping your symphony of employees, managers, and departments serve more smoothly and skillfully together. In a recruitment situation, these tuning forks can easily assess who will resonate with the culture and should be hired, and who is far off-key. That's why Google requires so many on-campus, in-person interviews for candidates with its already "Googley" employees.

Deeply loyal customers can become brand ambassadors and leaders of your culture, too. That's why Southwest Airlines involves its most loyal frequent flyers in final stages of new executive selection. This makes a powerful statement to both sides. To loyal customers it says that Southwest Airlines will only hire people who are absolutely dedicated to serving and delighting the customer. And to new employees this sends an even more unmistakable message: that they must be genuinely dedicated to uplifting customer service. After all, who made the final recommendation to hire you?

3. Ask Your Candidates to Get to Know Your Service

For real insight into your applicants' service mindset and understanding, ask them to experience your service, evaluate your competitor's service, and then make suggestions to improve your current service. If they can't see anything you might do better, you might be happy with their performance for a while. But if your candidate comes back with constructive ideas, or suggestions for a new best practice, you will be more successful—and for much longer—when that person joins your team.

4. Involve All of Your Staff as Recruiters

Your people already know and understand your service culture. Ask them to make recommendations of people they know, or who they have worked with in the past, who would be great additions to the team. That's why Starbucks gets and keeps so many successful new employees—because their current *baristas* are deeply involved in the local recruiting, screening, and selection process. Your best customers already know and appreciate your service. You can ask them for new hire recommendations, too.

5. Be Patient

Having a staff position vacant can be uncomfortable and costly. But don't let the "empty seat syndrome" drive you to fill that position with the wrong person too early. The impact of a misfit climbing onto your bus can make the ride unpleasant for everyone. And when that person ultimately quits, or stays on and others quit in frustration, you will go through another round of disappointment. You only want to hire the people who make your service culture even stronger. So ask yourself this question: "Will we be happy if we hire this person and they stay with us forever?"

Questions for Service Providers

- What are you doing to attract the best people to join your organization?
- How can you more actively participate in your organization's Service Recruitment process?

Questions for Service Leaders

- Is your recruitment process reliably selecting new team members who help to strengthen and deepen your service culture?
- What questions are being asked in your recruitment interviews? What other questions would help you identify candidates who are more perfectly aligned with your service vision and values?
- Who is involved in your Service Recruitment process now? Who else could you involve to make this vital process even more effective?

CHAPTER 10

Service Orientation

Your Service Recruitment Process worked like a charm, and now it is the first day at work for your new employees. How will you orient them to connect and contribute to your culture of uplifting service?

Unfortunately, many company orientation programs are far from uplifting. Often they are little more than robotic introductions: this is your desk; this is your password; those are your colleagues; these are the tools, systems, and processes we use; I am your boss; and if you have any questions, ask. Welcome to the organization. Now get to work.

OK, it isn't really that bad. Or is it?

Do you remember your first day or week on the job? Were you comfortable with all the new customers, colleagues, and expectations? Did the organization have a well-planned program to help you get connected, get settled, and get going? Did people go out of their way to make you feel wanted and welcome? If so, you know how much it means to someone new. If not, you know how much can be missing.

Basic inductions and introductions are important. New employees need to know where to go, what to do, and how things are supposed to work. But induction only gets them going on their job—it doesn't connect new employees to the company or the culture in a welcoming and motivating manner. You only get one chance to make a positive first impression with a new customer. Leading service organizations know the same is true with every new team member.

Service Orientation goes far beyond induction. Orientation provides valuable context as well as helpful content. It encourages good thinking and provides good answers for important questions like: Who are we? Who are our customers? Who are our competitors? How are we different? What's working? What's changing? What greater value can we create for our customers, our community, and for each other? What is the service culture we are committed to building here? And, most importantly, What can I do as a new employee to help make our service culture even stronger?

Zappos has gained global media attention for its four-week cross-department orientation process. It's an example of new-hire orientation at its finest—deeply embedding and delivering on the company's brand and core value, "Deliver WOW Through Service." Zappos pushes the process further by offering a "quit now" bonus during the four-week orientation process. If you think the culture isn't a perfect fit for you, the company will pay for the hours you've put in so far, plus a cash bonus to leave now with a smile. The bonus started at $100; was soon increased to $500, $1,000, $1,500; and now stands at a whopping $2,000 to walk out the door. And the CEO, Tony Hsieh, thinks the company might raise the amount again since not enough people are taking the money. You might say that paying new employees to walk away from the job is a little weird (which is another of their core values and is another reason why they do it), but this seemingly strange practice results in totally committed new team players who are completely aligned with the culture. The goal isn't to get rid of good people; it's to make sure the right people stay.

If the Zappos approach sounds wildly aggressive, that's because most organizations are simply crossing their fingers hoping new hires are happy. And that's too bad, because a simple online search of "effective orientation programs" reveals a flood of supporting statistics: effective orientation leads to greater productivity, higher employee engagement, longer staff retention, and better internal and external service. Clearly, the results are worth the effort.

You can focus your orientation efforts with these four proven steps: think and plan long term, connect your people and your culture, provide a reality check, and plan for continuous improvement.

1. Think and Plan Long Term

Effective orientation happens over time. New employees arrive with basic induction questions—How does the phone system work? Where do people meet and eat? When and how do I get paid?—and these should be answered quickly. After the initial settling-in phase, these questions will change and mature—How am I being appraised? How can I suggest changes and new ideas? and How can I get good guidance and support?

Avoid the temptation to "get it all over with" in one long and overwhelming session. Instead, stretch out the orientation process and encourage new employees to build their understanding over time.

For example, Marina Bay Sands begins an unofficial orientation process even before recruitment is complete. The resort hosts a colorful and interactive "Sands IQ" page on Facebook where job seekers can explore, and successful applicants can learn about, the many restaurants, hotel rooms, convention and exhibition halls, retail outlets, theaters, the museum, and other facilities located throughout the integrated resort. Applicants who want to grow their careers at Marina Bay Sands can demonstrate interest by learning important facts even before their first day on the job. And those who are hired can accelerate their orientation by visiting the Facebook page often and can contribute to new team member recruitment by sharing it with their friends.

By contrast, at Singapore Press Holdings (SPH), the media conglomerate that publishes many of the nation's newspapers, magazines, and online publications, a unique orientation program is available only for those who have already been in their jobs for at least six months. The SPH Management Orientation Program (SMOP) brings together team members from editorial, marketing, production, distribution, human resources, finance, facilities, IT, and other departments. Over five days, this diverse group learns how each job function has an impact on every other function. And they discover that only the whole team, working together and serving each other, can deliver the essence of its media brand: "Engaging Minds. Enriching Lives."

2. Connect Your People and Your Culture

At Changi Airport, new staff orientation includes every agency and company in the airport. Airline staff members meet employees from Starbucks, Billabong, Lonely Planet, and American Express. Cleaners, taxi representatives, and baggage handlers meet newly assigned members from Police, Customs, and Immigration. This combination breeds an intimate airport community where passengers are cared for across all job functions, employees respect all positions in the airport, and they begin to care about each other as if they were a large and well-connected family.

New employees are not the only ones touched by Service Orientation; managers, staff, peers, customers, suppliers, and even families back home are also affected. Each group has different questions and concerns that you can address by providing them with an active role in the orientation process. Buddy systems, lunch meetings, panel discussions, visits to other parts of the organization, family days, online portals, pages, conference calls, and virtual video meetings—you can use all these methods to *connect your people and your culture with your purpose.*

Seeing your name identified with an organization is critical for building connection. Make your new employees feel welcome with something that identifies they've officially joined your team: business cards, a name plate, a personal welcome letter from senior executives, a mention of their name in the company newsletter, their photograph on the intranet or website. At NTUC Income's award-winning contact center, new hires are asked to write a personal pledge to keep "Service Alive!" The following week, their pledges are proudly posted on the wall with photographs for everyone to see.

3. Provide a Reality Check

No workplace is perfect. Make sure your orientation is not a fantasy tour of what you wish the company would be. If your program shows only the bright side of the business and the happy side of daily work, don't be surprised if your new employees are disillusioned after a few weeks on the job. Before you send new hires out to love their jobs and serve the world, warn them of the realities they might face: burnout, rejection, and stress.

One technology firm in the middle of a wrenching transformation developed a new employee orientation program along the following theme: "You will know more about the problems we are facing today than some of the people who have worked here for years." This novel approach created new staff members who understood the past, who appreciated the present, and who were ready to contribute to make the future better.

And let's face it, sometimes it doesn't work out, and a new hire doesn't fit with the company culture. You may not offer $2,000 to walk away, but you can provide a dignified opportunity for new hires to leave after a short trial period if they choose. You might help them find appropriate positions in other firms you work with. Or give them honest advice about where to look for jobs that suit their manner.

It's always best to part as friends when people have shown sincere interest in your organization. They might apply for another position with you in the future. Or recommend a better-suited colleague to apply. Perhaps they will form an impression of what your organization is *really* like on the inside and share that widely on the outside. Whenever someone does not fit and leaves the job behind, they should know your culture cares enough to encourage them going forward.

4. Plan for Continuous Improvement

Orientation is your first opportunity to create open communication with new employees. Begin your working relationship by showing new hires that you will offer feedback and you want feedback from them. Don't let your orientation become a one-way stream of information. Let newcomers explore the company, research the competition, meet your customers—and then generate their own questions for you and your colleagues to answer.

You can also get your new employees more involved by asking them to help welcome the next batch of new employees with an even better experience. This ensures that your orientation program stays fresh and relevant. It also makes the group of new employees feel like valuable contributors: knowledgeable, involved, and useful.

Is all this effort worthwhile? Well, poor orientation of new employees can cost you dearly, because those who don't start right don't tend to stay long. And when they do leave, they don't speak well about your organization to others. And to top it off, high staff turnover means you must recruit, hire, and orient more new staff all over again. In new staff orientation, it pays to pay attention, and get it right the first time.

Questions for Service Providers

- What can you do to help new employees feel welcome and appreciated?
- How can you teach what you know best to the new people on your team?
- How engaging and effective was your Service Orientation when you started working? What suggestions can you offer to make it better?

Questions for Service Leaders

- Is your Service Orientation program for new employees welcoming, uplifting, and at the same time realistic?
- Do new hires complete your Service Orientation feeling engaged and eager to contribute?
- What changes will improve your current Service Orientation program?

CHAPTER 11

Service Communications

As customers of Stew Leonard's famous Norwalk, Connecticut, grocery store grab a shopping cart and head for the entrance, they know what to expect: an amazing atmosphere of music, color, the smell of fresh baked goods, and a world-class array of delicious food and drinks.

No visitor can miss the enormous slab of granite rock that bears this engraved message:

OUR POLICY

RULE 1: THE CUSTOMER IS ALWAYS RIGHT!

RULE 2: IF THE CUSTOMER IS EVER WRONG, REREAD RULE 1

This eye-catching, three-ton boulder makes a very public statement right at the front door, solidly reassuring every customer: "Don't worry. We will *never* argue with you." This sets the mood for confident and carefree shopping and sets an expectation of what the company will deliver.

And what does this massive chunk of stone communicate to every employee every day? "We know sometimes our customers are incorrect or they forget; they may exaggerate or even lie. But in this store we always give our customers the benefit of our full appreciation and the benefit of any doubt. Our customers may not always *be* right, but through our words and actions, we will always make our customers *feel* right."

Service Communications is the fifth building block in your uplifting service culture. This block includes how you make declarations about your service to everyone in your world, including your customers, partners, team members, media, industry, and community. The Stew Leonard's "Rock of Commitment" is an example of strong service communication, and it is one of many reasons why the store is so popular. It's even become a tourist attraction, with buses from New York City filling the parking lot each day. Your Service Communications also need to be rock solid, but may not be as weighty as a three-ton granite boulder.

At Westin Hotels and Resorts, you'll find something light, interesting, and unexpected engraved on the name tags of employees—the hobby or passion of each team member.

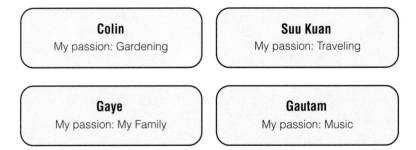

At first, these "passions" may not appear to be Service Communications. They don't instruct employees how to speak or interact with customers. They're not really actionable. They are just simple name tags—right? But what does every hotel want to cultivate with their guests? A preference, a repeat visit, a sense of loyalty, a connection. The Westin wants guests to feel comfortable connecting with its employees, and wants its employees to feel at ease communicating with each other. Can you think of a better way to create connection between two people than sharing a hobby or passion? With simple name tags as the catalyst, hotel staff members become approachable individuals who may have something in common with a hotel guest or with a fellow team member.

Compare this very personal approach with the very public ways Changi Airport communicates their nonstop dedication to uplifting service, internally to thousands of employees and externally to millions of passengers each year. To airport employees this communication begins the moment they pass through security each day. Huge posters are frequently refreshed with new expressions of the airport's service vision, photographs of top-ranked service personalities, winners of service contests, recipients of service achievement pins, and quotations from customer compliments. To passengers, Service Communications begin on the website, on arrival at curbside, or at the check-in counter. It continues inside the transit area, where beautiful banners promote the airport's success. But just in case you think the airport is tooting its own horn, the largest message by far is one of appreciation for passengers: "Your smile is our inspiration. Thank you for making us the world's most-awarded airport." What drives all this uplifting internal and external communication? Changi Airport's continuous commitment to providing personalized, stress-free, and positively surprising service.

At NTUC Income, the company launched and supported new service education courses with decals on the elevator doors. Every morning employees were greeted with this challenge: "Leap UP to the next level of service. Are you UP for it?" Standing on the street in front of the company building, you can't avoid the enormous and attractive orange signage. But colorful signage and new branding is not what made NTUC Income's revolution so successful. It was a comprehensive commitment to communicate, educate, lead, build, learn, and drive every member of the organization, and the organization itself, into a more uplifting service position.

The Medium Can Match the Message

Service Communications can be shown and shared in many mediums: signage, banners, plaques, pins and posters, formal meetings, informal events, town halls, brown bag lunches, online, off-line, mobile messages, video channels, login screens, e-mail signature files, screen savers, lunch-tray liners, notepads, manuals, checklists, dashboards and so much more. The opportunities are limited only by your imagination.

Don't stick your service message in some ancient format that no longer works. If the lunchroom is where conversations happen, put your service message on the walls, video screens, napkins, cups, and lunch trays. If people meet online to share and shape ideas, be sure the idea of uplifting service greets them there each day. Use whatever combination works for your company, your customers, and your culture.

Create on the Inside Before You Share on the Outside

Make private declarations early. Make public declarations only when you are ready. Promoting your service goals and aspirations is important for your team members. Uplifting Service Communications shows your employees and partners that they are part of something bigger than themselves, and may inspire them to make your cause their own. But shouting your service commitment to the world only makes sense when your team is fully committed and ready to deliver. People expect you to be accountable for your communications, to act on your word, and to back your declaration with authentic action. You can launch a service campaign on the inside when you are committed to make a difference. But only launch it on the outside when your customers will feel the difference.

Service Communications Are an Accelerator

Service Communications is a building block that can support every other element in the architecture of your service culture. Use Service Communications to promote your service language, expand your service vision, showcase your new hires, announce your latest contest, explain your measures and service metrics, and give voice to your customers' compliments and complaints.

Service Communications keep your people up-to-date with what's happening, what's changing, what's coming next, and most of all what's needed now. Service Communications can educate and inform, connect people and encourage collaboration, motivate, congratulate, encourage, and inspire.

Singapore Airlines publishes a monthly newsletter for its 14,500 employees called *Outlook* and a monthly magazine for its 18 million passengers called *SilverKris*. Both are rich with insights and up-to-date information. *Outlook* is essential to keep employees in 63 destinations in touch with the company and connected to their customers. One page in the newsletter is printed on a heavier stock of paper than all the others. This added weight indicates the page has great importance and makes it easier to keep, pass around, or pin up on the wall. The title of this vital sheet is "Transforming Customer Service." It's the focus that makes Singapore Airlines a consistent leader in airline profitability and awards. This page features stories about the employees who make the airline great and the actions they take to delight passengers and customers every day.

Questions for Service Providers

- Where can you find the latest information about your service, your customers, and your culture?
- How can you contribute to these communications and keep them up to date?

Questions for Service Leaders

- Are the Service Communications in your organization informative, engaging, and effective? Do they help communicate your plans and progress in the other building blocks?
- Do you personally participate in Service Communications?
- When was the last time you reviewed and refreshed your Service Communications? How frequently should this be done?
- Are you supporting innovation in this vital building block of service culture? What's next? What's new? What's uplifting?

CHAPTER 12

Service Recognition and Rewards

Paul McKenzie works in the fresh produce section in a grocery store. On his bright green apron is a large button that reads "I'm a Service Champion!"

Jenny Harman is a hair stylist with the longest list of loyal customers in her salon. Next to her work station is a crystal plaque that reads "Stylist of the Year."

Foo Teck Leong is an accountant who worked all weekend to help a client. His client was thrilled, and so was the owner of the firm. Teck Leong was given two box-seat tickets to an upcoming and bestselling show.

Vidya Kumaran is a sales executive for a software start-up. She recently visited an angry customer, solved a difficult problem, and landed a new contract that almost doubled her company's annual revenue. She was given a standing ovation from the entire company and an extra week's vacation.

Service Recognition and Rewards are a vital building block of service culture. They are a way of saying "thank you," "job well done," and "please do it again" all at the same time. Recognition is a human performance accelerator and one of the fastest ways to encourage repeat service behavior.

For many service providers, receiving a token monetary reward feels like an impersonal consolation prize—the easiest possible way to thank employees for their work, but also the least enduring. A well-known automobile dealership in Malaysia learned this lesson the hard way. It paid its sales team a special bonus for achieving high levels of customer satisfaction. But when bonus payments were curtailed during an economic downturn, customer satisfaction levels also fell.

Let's make this personal so you can feel the difference. Imagine you are hosting a dinner party and a guest arrives with a fragrant bouquet of flowers or a beautifully wrapped box of chocolates. A few days after dinner, the same guest follows up with a beautiful card and a handwritten note saying "Thank you." How would you feel about this person? Would you look forward to seeing this person again?

Now imagine a different guest arrives and hands you $20 in cash. This person suggests you buy yourself a bouquet of flowers, a box of chocolates, or anything else you like. A few days after dinner, the same guest sends you another $5. How would you feel about this? Would you look forward to inviting this person to dinner again?

Money makes a contribution, but heartfelt recognition makes a real connection. Genuine appreciation fully expressed makes a lasting impact on any employee. Gratitude from customers, admiration from colleagues, and strong approval from leaders of the organization—these can drive service commitment and behavior to even higher levels. Rewards are most effective when used as recognition: a special prize, a unique award, a bonus trip, an unusually uplifting event. These are more memorable and emotional than simply receiving money.

Everyone Responds to Recognition

Recognition can be given to your external service providers for their extra-mile efforts, outstanding service recoveries, greatest service improvements, or number of customer compliments received. Recognition can also be given to your internal service providers for upgrading their department's service, improving their procedures, streamlining their systems, or for their above-and-beyond efforts in helping each other succeed.

You can extend service recognition to everyone else in your community, too. Create an award for best service from a supplier, most appreciative customer, most helpful government agency, or even for your team's supportive family members at home.

The Many Ways to Recognize and Reward

Want your team to give better and more creative service? Then get better and more creative with your recognition and rewards. And there are so many ways! You can do it in public, in private, in person, in writing, for individuals, for teams, and with or without a physical or financial component. You can do it with a handwritten letter, a standing ovation, two tickets to a concert or a ball game, an extra day off, a box of specialty chocolates, dinner for the family, a large bouquet of flowers, a logo on the business card, a star on the name tag, a certificate of achievement framed on the company's wall of fame, a smiling photograph on your website. Recognition can even be as simple as a card like this that you print and pass along. I hand out hundreds of these cards to smiling service providers every month.

NTUC Income recognizes its contact center employees with paper stars and hearts on the wall—each with an employee's name and what an appreciative customer or colleague said about them. It's an ever-changing, always current "Hall of Fame" that uplifts everyone every day. Marina Bay Sands honors top employees by featuring their photographs and positive quotes on posters in the heart of the house. Singapore Airlines gives a coveted yearly award to staff members and teams who deliver on the company's highest aspiration: "Service even other airlines talk about."

American Express recognizes employees worldwide with an entire week that spotlights employee achievements on social networking sites. Arby's restaurants gets their customers involved in recognition by hanging a brass bell by the doorway with a sign that reads "If your service was GREAT, please RING the bell."

The National Eye Center has a unique approach to improving customer experience and boosting staff morale with recognition. In the main lobby is a prominent area called the "Staff Recognition Center" with complimentary letters from patients and their family members on display. Alongside each letter is a picture of the staff member cited and a certificate of appreciation signed by the managing director. Imagine how these staff members feel when they come to work each morning, knowing their customers and the organization appreciate them. Now imagine how other customers feel when they see these compliments on public display. They naturally anticipate receiving excellent service and they are more likely to express their appreciation when they get it. This is a win–win–win: the customer wins, the staff wins, and the organization wins.

Recognizing Your People
Rewards Your Organization

Does all this upbeat recognition and pat-on-the-back celebration really make a difference? Lanham Napier has no doubt. Napier is CEO of Rackspace, a leader in hosting and cloud computing services, famous for its promise to provide "Fanatical Support" and named as one of the "100 Best Companies to Work For" by *Fortune* magazine. Listen to what he says on YouTube about his "Rackers," the thousands of employees who keep the company's customers up and happy every day: "If you want really hard data, we track the engagement of our teams, and we look at productivity levels across different teams. On the days when we have an event or celebration, their productivity is 20 or 30 percent higher. It really renews the energy that Rackers are feeling about their work that day. So we know this stuff works."

Perhaps the ultimate recognition is being promoted to a new position of greater influence and responsibility within the organization. Those who are promoted should be role models of the service attitudes and behaviors you want everyone to follow. "At Schlumberger, promotion from within is one of strongest features of our global culture," says Stephanie Cox, the Vice President of Human Resources. "It is significant recognition for those who have exceeded expectations, provided great service to customers and colleagues, and demonstrated potential for contributing even more."

There is one more reason why recognition for service achievement should come frequently from an organization: because it doesn't come very often from customers. Imagine your service providers working overtime to calm angry customers, listening patiently to complaints, taking action, and following up to resolve every outstanding issue. When it's all over, how often do these customers say, "By the way, you did a great job of calming me down, listening patiently, and taking care of my concerns. Thanks. I really appreciate your terrific service?" The answer is—not often enough.

Providing service to others calls for our very best, and this kind of effort can be its own reward. But recognition from others is also uplifting and rewarding, and is well worth our best efforts.

Questions for Service Providers

- Do you participate in the service recognition programs where you work?
- How can you give praise to the colleagues who give you uplifting service?
- How can you express your appreciation to friends and family members who help support you and serve you at home?

Questions for Service Leaders

- Do you have an attractive and engaging set of Service Recognition and Rewards?
- Are your team members motivated and inspired by the rewards and recognition you provide?
- Are you personally involved in recognizing and rewarding your team members for delivering uplifting service?

Chapter 13

Voice of the Customer

Ready for a surprise?

At Changi Airport, even the washrooms can surprise and delight the most finicky traveler. Not only are the washrooms spacious and filled with soothing décor and music, but some of the women's washrooms also offer plush seating areas in front of large mirrors to spruce up before or after a flight. Across the hall, men are also surprised to find windows above the urinals, looking over the tarmac at aircraft taking off and landing.

What's not a surprise about the Changi Airport washrooms is the level of cleanliness. They are usually spotless, with every faucet and feature working correctly, every roll of toilet paper properly stocked, and every soap dispenser filled. That's because Changi Airport has integrated Voice of the Customer into a real-time, real-response system that ensures even the washrooms provide an optimal customer experience.

A computerized touch-screen in every washroom shows a photograph and the name of the washroom attendant. It also offers a timely greeting—good morning, good evening, or good afternoon—and then asks the traveler one simple question: "Please rate our toilet." Under the question are five large on-screen buttons with words and yellow faces, from a toothy grin for "Excellent" to a disappointed frown for "Very Poor."

The attendant and the maintenance office receive this feedback instantly when a passenger rates the washroom as "Poor" or "Very Poor." Immediately the attendant discovers and corrects whatever is not pleasant, not working, or not well-stocked. That's 42 million opportunities for actionable input from its customers every year. And that's only talking about the toilets.

Changi Airport knows the value of listening and responding to customers from all over the world. This is why there are so many active listening posts at the information counters, on the website, at the interactive kiosks located throughout the terminals, and most of all, through the eyes and ears of airport staff members who appreciate their customers' compliments, complaints, and suggestions. Airport team members don't get defensive when they hear a passenger's complaint because they know this precious voice has been the source of countless insights and innovations.

Changi Airport managers also listen keenly to the voices of their partners in service through interviews, roundtable discussions, and focus groups. They communicate closely with the Police, Immigration, and Customs departments, with airline representatives, and with the hundreds of vendors, suppliers, and tenants who create the Changi Airport experience every day.

Voice of the Customer is a valuable and powerful building block for improving your service culture. The voice of your customers can contribute immediately and powerfully to a better service experience. For example, keeping a washroom clean and attractive is relatively easy, since there is only so much that can go wrong.

But at Marina Bay Sands, more than 4,000 toilets and hundreds of thousands of other things can be temporarily out of whack. "We began collecting customer feedback immediately," said Tom Arasi of Marina Bay Sands. "When our doors opened and everyone was focused on simply operating for the first time, we knew that customer comments would be the fastest way to identify and address any problems. This was critical from our very first day of operations and it still contributes to our ongoing success."

How to Capture Your Customer's Voice

To find out what your customers really think and feel, start by genuinely asking for their feedback and suggestions. Many people have learned that standard surveys yield little response, and many dedicated hotlines are ice-cold. Make it clear that your customer's complaints, compliments, and comments will not only be collected and counted; they will be carefully studied, appreciated, and valued. Handing someone a customer feedback form is a request that is easy to ignore. But a vibrant program that says "Your Voice Counts!" "Tell us what you want!" or "We are listening to YOU!" is an invitation people will respond to.

Voice of the Customer is not a ranking, rating, or statistic. It is more qualitative than quantitative, and it is more of a subjective understanding than a purely objective measure. Voice of the Customer is the emotional commentary you need to study, and it is the expressive voice you want to hear.

For example, key drivers of satisfaction at Microsoft include product quality, value for money, security, accuracy, and speed of solutions. But that's not everything the company's customers and partners value. Microsoft carefully studies the millions of words and phrases people type into free-form comment fields every year.

Through careful analysis of these "verbatim" comments, the company discovered other drivers that also make a difference, including "Microsoft is easy to do business with," "Microsoft cares about me," and "Microsoft helps me grow my business."

You can capture the ideas, insights, and impressions of other people by asking questions like these:

- What did you like?
- What didn't you like?
- What would you like?
- What do we do that you really wish we didn't?
- What would you like us to change?
- What did you appreciate the most? The least?
- What should we start doing? Stop doing?
- What should we do more of? Less of?
- What could we provide that was missing?
- Did anyone or anything let you down?
- What could we do to win more of your business?
- What could we provide that would justify raising our prices by 10 percent?
- What are our competitors doing that you think we should do, too?

These questions open the door to active listening. But that's a long list of questions to choose from, and you might not want to ask them all. Choose the questions that work the best for you and for your customers. Then ask, listen, and learn.

San Diego International Airport applies this approach in a very simple manner with one large sign, a stack of attractive blue forms, and a collection box near the baggage claim carousel. The sign asks one big question: "How are we doing?" But the airport doesn't just want to know how they are doing; they want to know what they could possibly do better. Inside the form provided to capture passenger input is again, just one big question: "What can we do to make your next visit more enjoyable?"

Every member of your team can solicit Voice of the Customer feedback simply by asking, "Is there anything we can do better for you next time?" This accomplishes three important objectives. First, everyone on the team becomes an active listening point. Second, you gather new ideas at the very moment of delivery, when people's impressions and experiences are fresh. And, third, you automatically encourage customers to think about repeating business with you because you are asking how to serve them even better . . . the next time.

Finally, don't just ask for comments and recommendations; make a promise to respond with action. Let the people you ask know when their answers will be reviewed and when you will respond or make changes. If you are using an online form, an interactive interface, or a written comment card, you might add this line at the bottom: "May we reply to you personally about this? If so, please provide us with your contact details here." Now it's obvious that you are listening, taking action, making changes, reviewing, and replying to every comment every day.

The Joy of Customer Complaints

When things go wrong, customers complain. And that can be *good* for you and constructive for your organization because complaints can:

- highlight areas where your systems require improvement;
- identify where your procedures need to be improved, updated, or revised;

135

- reveal information that is lacking, is erroneous, or is simply out of date;
- identify team members who need more training or closer supervision;
- help highlight inconsistencies among shifts, departments, or locations;
- get important news and information straight to the top;
- educate everyone about what your customers experience and expect;
- help prevent complacency in a successful organization;
- help focus your attention, priorities, and budget;
- work as a trigger for new action, catalyzing positive change;
- keep you in touch with emerging trends and changing customer expectations;
- present new opportunities for raising revenue and solving problems;
- provide competitive intelligence by telling you what others are doing;
- identify which customers to invite into pilot runs, focus groups, and beta tests;
- give you content and current case studies for your service education programs; and
- provide feedback for you to publish, with your replies and action steps, in your Service Communications.

Most of all, complaints give you an opportunity to reply, respond, and win back customer loyalty. Most upset customers just walk away and complain about you to their friends and colleagues. The few who do speak up are giving you another chance. Take it.

Bringing the Voice Inside Your Organization

The messages you hear may be positive or painful, contented or upset, unsettling or energizing, upbeat or downbeat, distant or enthusiastic. What's important is that customers tell you how they feel. What's even more important is that you hear it.

> "Customer complaints are the school books from which we learn."
>
> *Lou Gerstner*
> *former CEO of IBM*

To harness the value of your customer's voice, share it frequently and widely throughout your organization. If the input you gather is all routed to one department where it's collected and then consolidated into a report, it won't have an immediate impact on your service or an emotional influence on your team.

At Marina Bay Sands, the comments gathered each day from guests are shared the very next day with team members in their briefings at the beginning of each shift. This brings a wealth of insight to those who can do something about it, by responding to suggestions, solving problems, and implementing new ideas.

The voices you gather may come through formal means such as survey forms, hotlines, comment cards and focus groups, or through social channels like Facebook, Twitter, Yelp, and TripAdvisor. Wherever it comes from, whatever it says, the value you gain from the Voice of the Customer is only achieved when this river of input connects with a team that wants to hear it, understand it, and do something about it.

This building block is called Voice of the Customer, but these approaches can also be applied to your colleagues, managers, staff, vendors, suppliers, distributors, partners, and even with your friends, neighbors, and family members. When we listen to appreciate and learn, when we take action to address the concerns of others, we are improving and uplifting the ways we live together.

Questions for Service Providers

- What have you learned from recent customer comments?
- What changes have you made—or can you make—based on customer compliments or complaints?

Questions for Service Leaders

- Are you personally involved in Voice of the Customer programs?
- How can you bring the Voice of the Customer to every member of your organization?
- What recent investments and improvements have you made based on your customers' compliments, complaints, and suggestions?

Tools *for* Your Journey	Get online companion tools FREE, including articles, videos, and easy to use guides revealing new ways you can take action now to begin uplifting your service today.
	www.UpliftingService.com

CHAPTER 14

Service Measures and Metrics

Leslie Jacobs relaxed in his seat as the long flight began to descend. He was on the tail end of a demanding business trip with too many meetings and not enough sleep. Leslie closed his eyes to enjoy a few precious moments of rest.

A tap on the shoulder jarred him. "Mr. Jacobs, would you complete this for us before we land?" He looked up as a member of the cabin crew handed him the airline's six-page passenger satisfaction survey. Before he could respond, the crew member walked back to the galley, leaving the survey in Leslie's hands. He saw rows of small text and columns with even smaller boxes. This was the last thing he wanted to do at the end of the flight. But he knew the crew would be waiting to collect it by the door so he pulled out a pen and started ticking boxes. The same crew member walked by and glanced nervously as Leslie completed the survey, as if any low marks might hurt him personally. The service on the flight was nothing special, but Leslie could feel the expectation, so he gave the crew members higher marks than they deserved.

That evening, a waiter at the restaurant asked if he enjoyed the meal. Leslie smiled with pleasure until the waiter pulled a satisfaction survey from his apron and handed it to him with the bill. Leslie sighed with resignation. It was another unwelcome form with too many questions seeking his opinion about everything from the quality of the food to the ambience, value for money, smiles, and speed of service. Dinner was delicious, but this last-minute task left a bad taste at the end of the meal, and he reflected that in the survey. The waiter noticed the low scores as Leslie left the table, and was confused.

Checking out of his hotel the next morning, the cashier handed Leslie yet another time-consuming survey asking him to answer questions about every aspect of his overnight stay. Leslie felt the hotel was good enough, so he marked "satisfied" across all the columns without any greater effort. Meanwhile, a Japanese guest checking out nearby was clearly delighted with his hotel experience and thanked the cashier profusely as he completed the same survey. Leslie noticed the overseas guest also checked "satisfied" all across the form, but did so with great enthusiasm.

The cashier didn't seem to care about either survey form. Both were unceremoniously dropped into a collection box, destined for a third-party vendor at the end of the week to wind up in another report at the end of the month, which made no difference at all to the cashier at the end of the day.

Sound familiar? This building block is called Service Measures and Metrics, and, unfortunately, many organizations use this building block quite poorly. Think of the last survey you were given at the end of a flight, a meal, or a hotel stay. Think of the last survey you were asked to complete online. Were you really glad to see it? Do you feel your responses made a difference?

Surveys are commonly used to measure satisfaction, assess loyalty, evaluate staff performance, and find areas for service improvement. But these evaluations are notoriously unpleasant for customers to complete and difficult for people in organizations to decipher. One problem is that surveys tend to grow longer over time and then become entrenched, generating self-sustaining rivers of data. Each new gathering of data must be matched against previous statistics, then be organized, interpreted, analyzed, and reported. But too often, committed service providers are left scratching their heads and wondering, "What does all this mean to us, and what should we do next?"

This process misses a vital point. Service Measures and Metrics are a valuable building block for service improvement. But to build a service culture, the methodology of these metrics must be uplifting for those you query and for the members of your team.

Clarify What You Are Measuring and Why

Just because you can measure many things doesn't mean that it makes good sense to track them all. What do you really want to know, and what action will you take with what you learn? Review this list and then decide which insights will be most helpful to improve your service now.

Customer Satisfaction: What are your customers' perceptions and expectations of your service? How satisfied are they with what you have delivered?

Customer Loyalty: How often do your customers buy from you? How often do they refer or recommend you? What is your share of their wallet? How connected do they feel to your service and your brand?

External Service Performance: Is the service you provide sliding, stable, or stepping up? Are you hitting your performance indicators and meeting service-level agreements?

Internal Service Performance: Is the service level inside your company going up or going down? Are your colleagues providing service to each other that accelerates or impedes the performance of your organization?

Employee Engagement: How strong are the attraction, retention, and motivation of your employees? Are they connected to your vision, to your customers, and to each other? Are they just employees on the payroll, or active evangelists working with a vision?

Staff Development: Are your team members progressing as professional service providers? Is your service education making any difference? Are your employees getting bored or getting better? Are they seizing every opportunity to develop their service skills and mindsets?

Don't Just Collect Data; Create Value

The purpose of this building block is to drive new actions that create and deliver greater service value. This purpose is perfectly aligned with our definition of service as *taking action to create value for someone else.*

Your actions can generate positive results in many different areas: performance, profitability, market share, reputation, customer loyalty, employee engagement, and more. Understanding the data can help you track progress, identify trends, and provide a baseline for future improvement. The right measures will also help you catch problems early and avoid pitfalls before they happen.

Service Measures and Metrics are most effective when they help you prioritize what's most important. What new commitments should you make? What new actions should you take? What can you do next, or do right now, to increase satisfaction, secure future business, or generate greater loyalty for your organization? If your current measures and methods of reporting do not achieve these goals, then it is time to review and revise.

Don't let your Service Measures and Metrics become disconnected from the practical levers of power. Collecting data and crunching numbers can easily become a separate function or a department, fueled by the urge to gather even more data and encouraged by the suppliers of surveys, facilitators of focus groups, and purveyors of mystery shopping. I am not against any of these practices; they all have their time, place, and function—so long as they lead you to new action.

Make sure the people on your team know what you are measuring and why. Be sure they understand which numbers you are tracking, and which needle you want them to move every day.

Make Your Survey a Positive Experience, Not a Painful Procedure

Your measurements process should feel like an opportunity to contribute, an invitation to help create a more satisfying experience.

People should look forward to participating in your surveys, interviews, and evaluations as a worthwhile investment of their time. If your current process is tedious, don't be surprised if only unhappy customers use it to tell you how upset they are. An unpleasant or unwelcome survey can destroy more value than it creates!

I recently flew into Kuala Lumpur, Malaysia, and had a wonderful ride in my hotel's car shuttle from the airport. The driver was so friendly. He gave me a cold towel and a cool drink. He offered a choice of music, talked about the weather, and made sure I was comfortable with the air-conditioning. His smile and good feelings washed over me during the drive, and I liked it.

At the hotel, I signed the guest registration and gave my credit card for payment. Then the counter check-in staff asked me to complete another form. It read:

LIMOUSINE SURVEY

Dear Mr. Ronald Andrew Kaufman:

To consistently ensure the proper application of our quality standard, we value your feedback on our limousine service:

Were you greeted by our airport representative?	YES / NO
Were you offered a cold towel?	YES / NO
Were you offered cold water?	YES / NO
Selection of music available?	YES / NO
Did the driver ask about the air conditioning?	YES / NO
Driver was driving at safe speed?	YES / NO

Room Number _____ Limo Number _____ Date _____

As I read the form, the good feelings fell away. The driver's enthusiasm suddenly seemed to be a charade. His concern for my well-being was just a checklist of actions to follow. His good mood was merely an act to meet the standard, not to connect with his guest. I felt like the hotel's "quality control inspector," and I did not like it.

If the hotel wants my opinion, they must make me an advisor, not an inspector. Ask me: What did you enjoy most about your ride from the airport? I'd have told them about their wonderful driver, and given him an A+. What else could we do to make your ride even more enjoyable? I'd have recommended providing a wireless tablet device with an Internet connection.

The Death of Customer Satisfaction

Every day, a quarter of the world's population connects via Nokia Siemens Networks' infrastructure, products, and solutions. The company serves telecommunications providers and partners in every corner of the globe with more than 70,000 employees throughout 150 countries. This giant business-to-business company knew very well that satisfying customers was essential for growth in profitability and market share.

But Nokia Siemens Networks had a problem: its Customer Satisfaction Survey was unwieldy. The survey had grown bloated, expanded over time to accommodate many internal requests for more data and details on customer expectations, perceptions, priorities, and competitive comparisons. It was like a bus with only 48 seats and 100 extra people hanging from every window, handle, rooftop railing, and bumper.

Customers did not enjoy this annual assessment process. Most ignored it. Many who did complete the survey used it as a hammer to hit the company hard with their complaints. Employees did not appreciate it either: it was difficult to decipher and hard to fathom what to do. Even worse, individual incentives were tied to very specific changes in one part or another of the survey, leading to individual actions that did not align well with each other across the organization.

"Imagine a customer satisfaction survey that consisted of 150 questions," says Jeffrey Becksted, at the time the company's Head of Customer Experience and Service Excellence. "We thought that the more information we could collect, the better we would be able to respond. But, imagine the effect of 80 thickly detailed PowerPoint presentations descending on our organization all at the same time. We simply had too much data for us to digest in a meaningful time frame. We were so focused on asking our customer about us, that we failed to ask the really important question of what actions we can take to create more value for them."

Managers at Nokia Siemens Networks knew there was a problem with the survey. "It was obvious that we had to take a fundamentally different approach to surveying our customers," Becksted says. "We were focusing on too many areas, and not asking action-oriented, value-creating questions. So, we started over."

Rajeev Suri, the newly appointed CEO of Nokia Siemens Networks, pulled the plug on this dysfunctional practice, and formed a new team to find a better way to measure. Imagine that for a moment. Here was a legacy process—built on years of adding and arranging questions to collect feedback for every department and process throughout the company—that generated massive amounts of data. And, overnight, the Customer Satisfaction Survey was gone.

How do you move beyond satisfaction? How do you stop looking backward to evaluate performance, and instead look forward to create new possibilities and potential? By changing your mindset—and transforming your survey—to a value-add proposition. Nokia Siemens Networks brought people from different departments together with a new goal—to create conversations and cultivate insights that would improve the relationships with their clients moving forward.

"Instead of asking clients how they rate our service, we asked them to explain their challenges, their goals, and the ways in which we could help them," says Becksted. "We asked them where Nokia Siemens Networks fits into their future—not how we've served them in the past. We asked about expectations and their experiences of working with us."

Today, instead of 150 questions focused on expectations, satisfaction, and competitive comparisons, Nokia Siemens Networks interviews its clients with a Customer Experience Survey that has far fewer questions and a greater focus on taking the right new actions, increasing loyalty, and building future business. And, they've already witnessed a tremendous response.

"It's a simple change," says Becksted proudly. "The question 'How did we do?' which is a lagging metric of past performance becomes 'What can we do?' which is a leading indicator of future success."

How can you move beyond satisfaction?

"Change the goal," says Becksted. "Companies don't put limits on process improvement, product development, and the bottom line. Why put a cap on improving service by simply reaching customer satisfaction? The goal needs to be constantly adding value. Focus on them, not you. Instead of asking a client to tell you how they perceive your service, ask them to tell you about their needs, challenges, desires, and goals. It doesn't matter how well you've done as much as it matters how they see you in their future."

"Get leadership involved," Becksted concludes. "If the leaders of an organization can't see the detriment of only measuring the past, then your company is doomed to become a thing of the past. However, if they can look into the future, and change the mindset and the survey, to move beyond satisfaction, the results can be astounding. It's a simple change that's already paying off for our company and our customers."

Reconnect to Be Responsible and Responsive

When you survey or interview customers, you create expectations that something will be done with their responses. Your process should close the loop to let them know that something has been done. The sequence looks like this: Conduct Survey → Capture Data → Conduct Analysis → Identify Insights → Take Action → Create Value → Repeat Survey.

If your customer says something should be changed in the first survey, you have an opportunity. If your customer says something should be changed in the first survey, and nothing has changed by the second survey, then you have a problem. Low scores in the first survey are acceptable; you want to uncover new opportunities for action. Low scores in the same area in the second survey can be dangerous if left unattended.

Service Measures and Metrics are a vital building block to help you identify problems, discover opportunities, drive new action, and create more value for your customers, your team members, and your organization. Will you settle for anything less?

Questions for Service Providers

- Do you understand what is being measured in your organization, and why these measures are important?
- Do you see how your own ideas and actions can help improve these measures?

Questions for Service Leaders

- Does your survey focus on collecting data or creating value?
- Does your current measurement process consistently lead to new improvement actions?
- Do your team members understand and act quickly on the information they collect?
- Is your survey a positive customer experience or a painful audit procedure?
- Do you reconnect with surveyed customers to thank them and inform them of new actions that have been taken?

CHAPTER 15

Service Improvement Process

Voice of the Customer will help you hear what your customers and colleagues want. Service Measures and Metrics will help you track what they need. This building block—Service Improvement Process—ensures you will create and deliver both.

Notice that the title of this vital building block is Service Improvement Process, not Service Process Improvement. A process improvement increases speed, reduces errors, improves efficiency, streamlines activity, or makes good use of a new technology. A Service Improvement Process is different; it is the methods and processes you use to challenge and support your people to continuously improve their service.

Wipro Ltd is a company of more than 120,000 employees based in Bangalore, India, a country with more than 1.2 billion people. In such an enormous pool of labor, standing out from the crowd is a challenge. Securing a certificate, credential, or document of achievement is one way of standing out, especially in a country with a long tradition of reverence for education. Wipro uses this to the advantage of its employees, its customers, and its culture with unique "X-Serve Projects" deployed across the organization.

In an ongoing company-wide campaign to improve customer-centricity, thousands of employees participate in customized classes of service education every year. After each class, Wipro prints—but does not distribute—personalized certificates bearing each employee's name. Although the employees have completed the class, and certainly want their "Uplifting Service Champion" certificates, Wipro holds the certificates back.

To receive these certificates of achievement, each Wipro employee must first complete a meaningful "X-Serve Project." First, the employee must take a specific new action that creates value for someone else—value that he or she has never delivered before. This action must demonstrate and apply the fundamental principles of customer-centricity that were taught in the class. But even then, the certificates are withheld.

Next, after the employee takes new service action, he or she must obtain a written message from the person served. This message must confirm the action taken and, more importantly, the value received. Finally, with this confirmation of action taken and added service value, Wipro proudly awards these certificates to their "Uplifting Service Champions."

Wipro's "X-Serve Projects" are a terrific example of an effective Service Improvement Process: a proven method ensuring each employee effectively puts new concepts into action . . . at least once.

But one successful application of new learning is not enough, so Wipro created another Service Improvement Process. They launched a contest called "Value I Added," which can only be entered by individuals or teams that deliver greater value to Wipro customers than the customers requested, expected, or even paid for. In 2010, this contest attracted over 1,800 entries, with winners and their projects capturing the attention and admiration of the whole organization.

These two processes—"X-Serve Projects" and the "Value I Added" contest—connect learning with action and challenge employees to deliver added value. But Wipro also wants to enroll its customers in building the company's culture. So it created yet another improvement process by including a unique question to its customer satisfaction reviews: "What value have we *added* since the last time we met that was not promised to you at our last meeting?"

What a remarkable question! Wipro intentionally asks customers to identify value received *beyond* any existing contract or service level agreement. Consider the impact on the Wipro employees who know this question will be posed to their customers. What would your customers say in response to such a question?

"The challenge we faced was to get people to develop a service mindset and constantly look for ways to improve the experience for external customers and internal colleagues," says Usha Rangarajan, General Manager of Mission Quality & Wipro Way (Wipro's Business Excellence Framework). "By institutionalizing our service philosophy of being 'proactive, value-adding service partners' into the process of service education, contests, recognition and rewards, we have created a measurable improvement in our customers' experience."

What Is a Successful Service Improvement Process?

A Service Improvement Process creates focus. It keeps the spotlight on service improvement and builds passion for elevating service.

This is not a onetime thing that people may or may not notice. It's a continuous progression of issues, questions, projects, and invitations connecting people with your vision and committing them to service improvement.

This building block drives service innovation. It's the crucible in which competition powers creativity and stubborn problems meet out-of-the-box solutions. This is where customer complaints are wanted and welcome, where survey reports are carefully examined for new ideas and insights.

Service leaders know that competitors are always snapping at their heels or already stepping out ahead. To gain a sustainable advantage, you must deliver more value today than you did yesterday, and even more tomorrow. A Service Improvement Process keeps focus and attention on this goal.

A Service Improvement Process creates synergy by connecting people between levels and functions. Some issues require ownership on the front line, involvement from the middle, and sponsorship from above. Other service issues are quickly solved by teams working across silos. Cross-functional team members bring new perspectives and fresh energy to old problems.

A well-designed Service Improvement Process promotes communication across functions, divisions, and departments. It stimulates collaboration across levels, languages, and locations. With thoughtful planning and invitations, you can also tap the creative energy of your customers, vendors, distributors, and even your government or industry regulators.

Your Service Improvement Process may include many different methods. You can use the following approaches, create new ones, combine old ones, and change any you are using over time. Your constant challenges are to focus attention, gain active participation, and generate real results.

Problem-solving workshops: Albert Einstein said, "Problems cannot be solved by the same level of thinking that created them." Elevating an issue from daily difficulty to a dedicated workshop also graduates that problem—and the people working on it—to a higher level of thinking.

Cross-functional teams: Sometimes the best ideas come from those who aren't closest to the problems. The participants on cross-functional teams not only learn to understand the concerns of other departments, but they also bring fresh energy and perspectives.

Job rotations: Do you know what it's like to wear someone else's shoes for a day? Try it, and let your employees try it, too. The first question from people reporting to new departments is typically, "Why do you do it this way?" And that's often followed by, "Wouldn't it work better if . . . ?"

Service improvement contests: Many people are motivated by a challenge to win. If your team responds to competition, create a structure that harnesses this drive for the benefit of those you serve. When service improves for customers on the outside and for colleagues on the inside, then people serving on all sides will feel like winners.

Sharing best practices: Sharing effective examples and successful stories can educate, motivate, and inspire. Find out what is working well inside your organization and then spread the news with online stories, brown bag lunches, weekly meetings, town hall events, formal case studies, and personal interviews and conversations.

Applying new technology: Technology offers many possibilities to measure, deliver, accelerate, and refine. To apply technology as a Service Improvement Process, frequently ask: "How can we use technology to support our service providers? How can we liberate their time and spirit to do what only people can do—caring and responding to the concerns of other people."

Keep Your Process Fresh and Flowing

After you discover which methods work best for your culture, keep them fresh by changing the criteria, timing, reward, or any another aspect of your programs. When you want people to improve what already exists, it helps to put a little madness in the method. For example, no one ever hung a suggestion box hoping it would be ignored. But rarely will a mere suggestion box attract a healthy flow of good ideas. Now imagine a staff suggestion program that captures attention with a different service challenge and a different form of recognition every month:

January: Submit your best ideas for welcoming our new customers. Winners celebrate with dinner for two at a fancy restaurant.

February: Submit your best ideas for appreciating our loyal customers. Winners receive a one-year subscription to a useful publication of their choice.

March: Submit your best ideas for improving service between two or more departments. Winners from both departments get tickets to an upcoming show.

April: Submit your best ideas for speeding up a service process. Winners receive a brand new pair of running shoes.

May: Submit your best ideas for bouncing back with service recovery when something goes wrong. Winners get an extra day off.

June: Submit your best ideas for reducing costs while maintaining or improving our service. Winners take home a percentage of the savings.

July: Submit your best ideas for increasing our sales through service. Winners attend a training program of their choice.

August: Submit your best ideas for recruiting new team members who live our values and are motivated by our purpose. Winners enjoy a deluxe buffet with our next batch of new recruits.

September: Submit your best ideas for benchmarking other organizations. Who should we visit and why? Winners join the group that goes on the benchmarking visit.

October: Submit your best ideas for collaborating more closely with our vendors. Winners get a behind-the-scenes tour at the vendor's organization.

November: Submit your best ideas for keeping our customers' needs and interests top of mind. Winners are invited to follow any senior leader of the company for a day.

December: Submit your best ideas for new topics for our monthly suggestion program. Winners will see their ideas put into action next year.

Questions for Service Providers

- Do you participate enthusiastically in a Service Improvement Process?
- What service problems do you think could be resolved with your organization's Service Improvement Process?

Questions for Service Leaders

- Is everyone on your team fully engaged in a Service Improvement Process?
- Do your team members feel motivated and empowered by the improvement processes you use?
- How do you personally support service improvement workshops, initiatives, contests, and suggestion programs?

CHAPTER 16

Service Recovery and Guarantees

You're on the edge of your seat, fingers crossed, teeth clenched. You don't know what's going to happen next. The anticipation is so thick you can smell it, taste it, and feel it. You are watching one of the great comeback moments in a classic movie. Nothing is more captivating than an underdog who triumphs in the end.

Hollywood loves the underdog. It's a formula for box-office riches: the ragtag team that wins the championship, the quirky guy who gets the girl, the unexpected hero who saves the day. This magic formula works in business, too. It's a formula that will uplift you, your customers, and your organization. And it all starts when you are at your worst, in the moment after you've made a mistake. Yes, this building block begins when you are the underdog in the eyes of your customer.

No matter how much you prepare and improve, things will go wrong from time to time. Expectations will drop, customers will be disappointed, and some team members may even feel ashamed. Others, to avoid being blamed for causing the problem in the first place, might scurry away while pointing a finger at someone else. In some cultures, bad news is unwelcome and denial is the norm. It doesn't have to be that way.

Bouncing Back with Service Recovery

Consider Xerox Emirates, a Dubai-based joint venture of the prestigious global document-management company. By 2006, the company was already a three-time national quality award winner and a leader in market share and profitability. It was well known for operational excellence, but not yet for service excellence. Xerox Emirates wanted to claim that position in the minds of its customers, its competitors, and its team.

The company launched a vigorous service-culture-building program with every team member learning the service principles you will discover in section 4. The first year, its engaging service vision was "Better Than Expected." According to customers' feedback, this vision was successfully achieved. The second year, Xerox Emirates revised the vision upward to "Much Better Than Expected." In the third year, with the service culture strong and supportive, the company turned to occasional complaints as a source of competitive advantage.

Xerox Emirates already had an in-house service initiative called the Customer Care Management System, a software program for tracking customer complaints. But the thinking behind the system was flawed. "It was used reluctantly," says Andrew Hurt, the General Manager. "Employees viewed the system as a tool for leadership to blame someone for poor service performance. In fact, many feared putting complaints into the system because it could lead to personal recrimination."

Think about it. Would you log a complaint into a system if it might get you into trouble? Xerox Emirates employees were hiding complaints, doing all they could to avoid the system, conveniently forgetting dates and details, quashing the voice of valuable customers who had real problems and needed to be heard the most. The result was a blind spot and a weakness—a misaligned element in the culture.

How would this play out in an iconic comeback film? That's easy, right? In the movie, Team Xerox Emirates would use its shortcomings as an avenue to build up winning strength. In the script, the biggest shortcoming would become the distinctive move that wins the game. And that's exactly what Xerox Emirates did. (Remember the winning kick in *The Karate Kid*?)

"We killed the old system and launched a new program called *Bounce!* as our service-recovery tool," says Hurt. "Instead of blame and shame, we presented shortcomings as an opportunity to elevate our service. Like a ball dropping, we could ignore it or we can work hard to make it bounce by raising the level of our service much higher than it had been to start. Not only could we learn from mistakes and fix them, we realized that complaints were a great opportunity to surpass expectations because we were being told the specifics of our clients' frustrations."

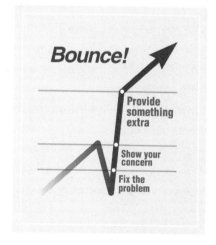

The goal of *Bounce!* is very simple. Imagine a customer's perception of your products and service as if it was a bouncing ball. The ball originally rests in your hand. When it's dropped, the customer's perception of you is declining. When it hits the floor, the perception has bottomed out—in the eyes of your customers, you are at your worst. If you only fix the problem, that's a basic level of service and the ball comes up a bit. But if you work on the recovery like a special opportunity, you have a chance to bounce the ball much higher. You can surpass your original position with a perception of surprising service—and this opportunity never would have happened without something going wrong.

Your Mission: Find and Solve Complaints

Hurt says that once the team members at Xerox Emirates realized that they had an opportunity to excel—and were assured of management support—they began actively searching for problems. The term *personal responsibility* took on a new meaning. Accolades were given to those team members who discovered hidden customer problems or created innovative ways to recover favor with upset customers.

The *Bounce!* measure of success was innovative, too. After a problem was discovered and recovery action taken, the customer was asked just one question: "As a result of what happened and what we have done about it, are you now more or less loyal to Xerox Emirates?" This question concentrates attention on restoring a customer's confidence in the company. And it caused the company to put an even greater focus on understanding the preferences of each customer. Instead of a standard product replacement or service recovery discount, the company started paying much closer attention to who was actually inconvenienced or upset—and to figuring out what these people valued.

For example, one upset customer had been eyeing a new color all-in-one device, but could not muster the budget. Xerox Emirates loaned him the machine for two months and paid for all the toner used. The customer was delighted—and two months later managed to find the budget. Another frustrated customer supervised a large team of frontline staff. A big box of chocolates courtesy of the company put sweet smiles on them all. And then there was the customer who felt disturbed that no one would really listen to his problems. Managers knew from previous sales calls that he was an avid weekend golfer. After two friendly rounds of 18 holes with company leaders, he felt appreciated and understood.

In each case and hundreds more, the company followed up with this question: "As a result of what happened and what we have done about it, are you now more or less loyal to Xerox Emirates?" You can guess the answer.

Here's the most interesting part of this comeback story. Because Xerox Emirates managers now focus on achieving the recovery outcome instead of blaming the source of the problem, employees stopped being afraid when things go wrong. In fact, managers praise team members who bring dissatisfied customers to their attention. Rather than ignore customer complaints or try to cover them up, employees see them as opportunities to be recognized and excel. While the number of complaints logged into the *Bounce!* system has increased substantially, the company's "satisfaction with service recovery" scores have also risen dramatically.

Today, Xerox Emirates is taking this approach even further, sending teams into customer sites specifically to hunt for problems. Unlike a typical quality control audit or satisfaction-confirming visit, the company intentionally seeks the negative. Teams hunt to discover when, how, and why machines break down. Teams focus on how often and how quickly customers need assistance. Teams focus on problems that could arise with customer communications, delivery, maintenance, and education. They actively solicit complaints from customers—each one is an opportunity to *Bounce!* "This year's target," says Andrew Hurt, "is another 300 percent increase in complaints." How would you like to compete against a company with a recovery policy and a service culture like that?

Building Your Service Recovery System

No one has a perfect record when it comes to delivering service. You will have unhappy customers, and you will receive complaints. With social networking, viral videos, and bad news traveling fast, one angry customer can leave a lasting stain on your reputation. Your recovery policy and practices should be ready.

1. **Get senior management support.** Unlike routine aspects of business, service recovery requires acknowledging mistakes and doing whatever it takes to recover. This often means going outside normal procedures, deliberately bending the rules, and possibly spending money in the process. Therefore, this building block needs understanding and encouragement from the top.

2. **Practice your recovery plan.** When things go wrong is not the time to think about how to recover. The clock starts ticking the moment a problem occurs. SWAT teams are successful because they anticipate scenarios and run practice drills long before something dangerous happens. Run your own scenarios to imagine what could go wrong. Then communicate your plans, test your tactics, and rehearse your responses in advance.

3. **Go hunting for service problems.** Be aggressive and proactive. Create discovery systems that seek out breakdowns and complaints. It may not feel good to spotlight your flaws,

but view service recovery as a disease-prevention formula and you'll catch problems long before they make you sick.

4. Empower frontline staff. Give those closest to the issue the power to make things right. The Ritz-Carlton Hotel famously empowers every employee with a substantial recovery fund to delight guests when something is wrong, without a moment's delay. The analysis and insights can come later. The actions to recover are needed right away. Nothing frustrates an upset customer more than hearing this: "I'd really like to do that for you, but I have to check with my manager first. It should only take a few days."

5. Go for the big win–win! We love great comeback movies because the underdog comes from behind to surpass everyone's expectations. Your recovery strategy should strive to do the same. The goal is not just fixing problems; it's creating experiences that unexpectedly delight. And great comeback stories are the ones people love to share. When your customers win, your company wins, too.

6. Lock in the gains. You can get much better at anticipating new problems, faster at detecting current problems, and create better tools and training to bounce back whenever a ball is dropped. Create a program in your organization where stories of recovery are collected, and service providers are recognized and rewarded. Analyze each story carefully, because some will reveal how to prevent mistakes in the future or delight customers with uplifting service before a mishap ever happens.

Growing Your Business with Service Recovery

Customers who struggle with a service problem have been to a low point with you. And when you recover, they experience bouncing back. This experience of disappointment followed by relief can actually increase customers' confidence in your service. Why is that? Because everyone knows that problems will occur from time to time. Things break down in life, difficulties arise, and unpleasant things do happen. What we don't know is how any service provider will respond in these situations until they happen.

When a problem does occur and successful recovery follows, you learn something important about a service provider that you couldn't know before. Now you know, from personal experience, this service provider can be trusted to do the right thing when you really need it. This added confidence leads to customers coming back, thereby increasing their value to the service provider. Repeat customers tend to buy more, and often are the first to try your premium offers. These people also recommend you with a real-world legitimacy that cannot be purchased with advertising. Every customer with a problem is your potential admirer and evangelist—when you successfully recover.

An additional upside of service recovery can be found inside your organization. When your organization has a track record of doing the right thing in problem situations, then every member of your team can serve with confidence and pride. Knowing your organization will always bounce back up is a powerful reason to feel good when you are serving, and when you are recovering.

What's the alternative? What are the consequences if this building block remains weak and mired in the problematic procedures of rebates and returns? Team members get frustrated and embarrassed, or, even worse, cynical and resigned. Customers get stuck in negotiations, calculations, and other distractions from the goal. These frustrations turn into unpleasant stories, the bad news that travels fast, the tales of woe that people always love to tell and often exaggerate along the way. Who listens to these stories? Their friends, your customers, prospects, competition, and anyone else with an interest and an Internet connection or a need to buy whatever it is you sell. That may not be an easily quantified impact, but it's costly to even consider.

How Generous Should You Be?

With so much at stake, how much should you give away? Many companies invest heavily in advertising, promotions, and introductory offers to attract new customers. Yet they resist allocating a generous slice of their budget to service recovery. It seems like money spent on marketing leads to more new sales and profits, while money spent on service recovery looks like profits earned are now being lost. This is a flawed and dangerous way of thinking.

Recovering an existing customer is often much less expensive than is attracting and acquiring a new one. Existing customers have already gone through the process of signing up, logging in, or whatever else it takes to be your customer. They have already made an investment of time and money, and they want that investment to deliver as you promised. When you keep your promise in a recovery situation, loyalty deepens quickly and the lifetime value of customers begins to grow.

Think about it. A young married couple buys their first refrigerator from an appliance retailer, a high-end model from a prestigious overseas brand. The unit is delivered to their home. Everything is fantastic, except a decorative piece of the door handle is missing. The delivery team calls the store, and it is informed that a replacement piece can be specially ordered and would arrive in two to three months. The young couple asks if they could get the piece from another unit already in the store. But the store manager declines, stating, "Then we'll have a piece missing from our inventory." This may sound like a minor flop, but consider the lifetime value of a young couple just starting to buy household appliances. They'll want a laundry machine, a dishwasher, a microwave, and a vacuum, among other appliances. And every recently married couple knows other recently married couples.

Now imagine the store manager learns of the problem and promises to replace the refrigerator later the same day. And when the delivery team members arrive, they also bring two shopping bags full of tasty treats purchased from the supermarket.

It looks like the profits from the sale of that refrigerator were just spent on groceries, and that is true. But where do you think this young married couple will buy all of their other appliances? How many times will they delight in telling this story to their friends? How often will they recommend this store to others? What mood will they be in every time they visit the store? And how will the store manager and the delivery team feel about their jobs, their company, and their commitment to bouncing back? Giving your customer a little bit more doesn't mean you lose. In the end, you can gain a lot.

Resources invested in service recovery come back multiplied through the network of people you serve. And some recovery resources cost you no money at all. You can also bounce back by giving people more attention, making personal contact, providing better follow-up, offering additional training, extending an existing warranty, or simply delivering a higher level of genuine concern and care.

Uplifting Service—Guaranteed?

When you know your team and culture can bounce back and recover, take the next step and make it guaranteed. A guarantee is not only an assurance that things will go right—it's a promise that you will make things right if they ever do go wrong.

Consider the way Lexus promotes its service contracts and guarantees maintenance of its vehicles. Drivers worldwide have come to expect and appreciate that their Lexus service department stands behind their products and will recover quickly whenever a problem occurs. Lexus doesn't know what might go wrong, but it's committed to maintaining a reputation for service as admirable as the quality of its cars. That requires systems, people, and a passionate service culture eager to solve problems and guarantee satisfaction.

There are three key questions to ask yourself when preparing to launch your guarantee.

1. Is Your Guarantee Meaningful?

Just as recovery must be fast to be effective, a guarantee must be meaningful enough to make your customers happy. We've all heard pitches that promise, "If you're not happy, we'll give your money back." That works to sell products, but a money-back guarantee doesn't always work to keep your customers. Imagine you buy a refrigerator and for some reason it doesn't work well. The food spoils, you get sick, and now you're angry. Even if the company gives your money back, will you buy an appliance from that store or that product line again? If a hairstylist gives you a horrible haircut, will you go back to the same salon just because it returned your money? Service guarantees can't just focus on equal bartering. Great guarantees promise if something goes wrong, a customer will experience happiness, not just an exchange or return of value.

Guarantees must be flexible to be effective. Many companies create standard policies for service and product replacement when things go wrong. But it's important to listen and respond to each upset customer as an individual. For example, a restaurant may have a policy that empowers servers to offer complaining customers a free dessert. That may suffice if a customer is unhappy because he or she ordered salad with dressing on the side, but it came with the dressing poured on top. But what if the hostess was rude, or the waiter spills coffee on a customer's business attire? A piece of cake isn't meaningful recovery in these situations. Greater flexibility and empowerment are required.

2. Is Your Guarantee Easy to Collect?

A guarantee must be easy to invoke, redeem, or collect. Don't make the initial offer if you are going to frustrate your customer with a convoluted process. I recently subscribed to an online service because I was interested in the generous offer. It was priced at a great introductory rate, and the guarantee stated that I could stop the membership at any time. But when I tried to unsubscribe, I couldn't reach anyone by phone. The response to my emails was even more disturbing, asking for "A written letter of discontent stating the reasons why you do not want to continue your membership," with a small disclaimer that read "Your letter must be received and approved four weeks before termination of your subscription."

By contrast, years ago I lived in an area of the world with cold winters and great skiing. I bought a pair of silk long underwear by mail order from L.L.Bean, a company legendary for its service and its lifetime guarantee. The silk was smooth and comfortable, and the underwear kept me warm. Then I moved, and moved again, and found myself 20 years later unpacking boxes in the equatorial city of Singapore. And there were the silk underwear. They were not much use to me now, and not even attractive because they had holes in the knees and were fraying at the ends. I almost threw them away.

Then I remembered L.L.Bean's lifetime guarantee, and on a lark I put the underwear in a plain, brown envelope and inserted a simple handwritten note: "Please replace these. Thank you." I didn't even have the company's address, so on the outside of the envelope I wrote: "L.L.Bean, Customer Service, Maine, USA." At the post office, I felt foolish mailing back such a ragged piece of clothing. It didn't seem right to send old underwear all the way around the world by airmail. So for just a dollar, I sent them off by sea.

Time passed and I forgot all about it. Life filled with new sports and new underwear. Then, two months later, an envelope arrived from L.L.Bean. Inside was a money order for one dollar and no explanation, just a dollar. I figured they evaluated the old clothing and somehow calculated its leftover value. I shrugged, and laughed, and soon forgot about it.

Another month passed and another envelope arrived. Inside was a brand new pair of long underwear the same size and color as my old ones. Several months later I called L.L.Bean to place a holiday order for some relatives. Chatting with the representative, I told her the story of my underwear. "One thing still confuses me," I confessed. "What was the one-dollar money order for?" She replied, "Before replacing your underwear, we wanted to refund your postage."

L.L.Bean is very public about its promise of satisfaction. They call it "Guaranteed to Last," and it reads like this: "Our products are guaranteed to give 100% satisfaction in every way. Return anything purchased from us at any time if it proves otherwise.

We do not want you to have anything from L.L.Bean that is not completely satisfactory." This guarantee is simple, meaningful, and powerful! Is yours?

3. Are You Ready to Launch Your Guarantee?

When should you take your promise to the world and announce your guarantee? You think you might be ready, but are not 100 percent sure. Some will recommend you wait, make sure all possible scenarios are covered and systems are in place. Be sure everything and everyone is ready. The problem is—you may be waiting a very long time.

The best time to launch an uplifting service guarantee is when you are close but not yet perfect. The final keys to a stellar performance appear when a show goes live, not in the last stages of rehearsal. A magic sparks to life when your guarantee is on the line and real customers come calling. Problems will appear that you do not foresee, no matter how much you plan. Breakdowns in your system will crop up and lead to breakthroughs, which is exactly what you want. And the cost of early recoveries while your guarantee stabilizes is small change compared to the big change in the quality of experience your customers will enjoy and the excitement your team members feel.

Service Recovery and Guarantees Delivers Lifelong Value

The goal of this building block is not to create one positive experience or one loyal customer. The goal is to create a culture that earns and retains many loyal customers while building pride and problem-solving passion in every service provider. Confidence is the key. When customers are confident about the service you deliver, they will return, refer, and recommend. When team members are confident about your commitment and your culture, they will work enthusiastically to deliver uplifting service.

Is this building block a good place to invest your time and money? Effective service recovery turns upset customers into loyal advocates. Guarantees turn team members into true believers. The results you gain are worth the effort. And that promise is guaranteed.

Questions for Service Providers

- What are your recovery policies and procedures?
- What can you do to quickly recover when something does go wrong?
- What problems can you anticipate? What solutions can you prepare?

Questions for Service Leaders

- Do your people actively seek problems as opportunities to bounce back?
- Do your team members bring problems to you eagerly or hide them quickly?
- Do you have a robust budget for service recovery? Is it easy for people close to the problem to provide an immediate solution?
- Do you offer a meaningful service guarantee? Should you?

CHAPTER 17

Service Benchmarking

Imagine you drive into a parking lot and find that the most convenient space has been reserved for your arrival. Someone approaches your car and holds the door open as you step out. He introduces himself and guides you toward a small security counter. The security guard greets you personally. A badge with your name has already been prepared. Beyond security you find a red carpet leading you into the building.

The meeting room is comfortable and well prepared, with presentations neatly arranged on the table. A selection of refreshing drinks is available to suit your taste. As you take your seat, a small gift is given to you by one of the smiling hosts. Inside the elegant box you find a modern, attractive pen engraved with your full name. As you thank your hosts, they smile and nod respectfully to you in welcome.

Where are you? In the conference room of a private bank? In an elegant showroom for luxury goods? In a jeweler's special enclave for celebrities and other wealthy guests?

It may be hard to imagine, but you have arrived for an on-site visit at a Vopak terminal in Asia. Vopak is the world's oldest and largest provider of conditioned storage facilities for bulk liquids, and is an emerging icon of uplifting service. With 80 terminals in 30 countries—storing liquids and gaseous chemicals, oil products, petrochemicals, biofuels, vegetable oils, and liquefied natural gas—you might assume that the company is more focused on safety and operational excellence than it is on the aesthetics and emotional appeal of service. But your assumption would be wrong.

Vopak certainly understands the necessity of safety and the value of operational excellence, and it works hard to maintain its excellent reputation in both of these areas. But Vopak is also working hard to differentiate itself with service before this becomes the new industry standard. Vopak knows its competitors aren't yet providing uplifting service. And it is looking outside its own industry to learn how other organizations have built lasting reputations for world-class levels of service.

What Is Service Benchmarking?

Standard business benchmarking means comparing your business processes with the best practices of selected "target" organizations. Dimensions frequently studied include quality, time, and cost—with an eye toward improving your own processes to increase output, reduce waste, boost speed, or lower costs.

As a building block of service culture, Service Benchmarking is distinctive. First, when you explore the dimensions to study, focus on service experiences, not just processes. How do leaders in other fields create service value, increase customer loyalty, deepen service partnerships, improve internal service, and build a service culture where great people love to work?

Second, your objective is not only to improve your processes and results. As a building block of service culture, an equally important goal is creating endless curiosity throughout the organization with every person observing, inquiring, and learning. Your objective is a self-sustaining culture distinguished by uplifting service, not just valuable data points for tactical service improvements. You want to develop a focused team of service providers who seek to understand: How do other leaders create uplifting service experiences for their customers and colleagues? What can we learn, then adapt, adopt, and apply to improve the service we deliver to our customers and to each other?

Benchmark the Experience

Benchmarking opportunities exist at every point in the customer experience: discovering, shopping, testing, trying, buying, applying, learning, improving, upgrading, installing, and even commenting, complaining, and returning.

I worked with a global team of Microsoft Operations leaders at a global conference to improve their customer and partner experience. They were conducting an early benchmark discussion about who to study for best practices in their field. With an ordering system that includes authorization, activation, security assurance, credit checks, license updates, and billing approvals, the company naturally thought about other large software licensing organizations with similarly complex systems: SAP, Oracle, IBM, Cisco, and others.

I offered that the fastest benchmark they could apply was Amazon's patented "1-Click" system. One of the leaders quickly responded with an explanation about how business-to-business purchases through a partnership channel are completely different from someone buying a book for delivery to his or her home or for downloading to his or her Kindle.

"It's not what is being ordered that I suggest you benchmark here," I said. "It is the process for placing the order." The executive paused quietly for a moment, thinking about how many different screens his partners must navigate to successfully place their orders. Then he nodded, recognizing the challenge that lay ahead and the benefit of benchmarking Amazon.

You can benchmark any point in the customer experience. For example, who does a terrific job with their newest customers, making them feel welcome, comfortable, and successful? The new car delivery process at the BMW factory in Germany is so uplifting that people schedule their purchase months in advance and fly in from all over the world. What is it like to be a brand new customer of your organization?

Who takes terrific care of existing customers, earning a high rate of returning customers and low volume of product returns? Apple is a leader in personal devices with levels of loyalty earned at the Genius Bar in their stores every day. My daughter, Brighten, smiled as they replaced her laptop battery for free. She said, "I don't know why anyone with an Apple would ever switch to another brand." Do your customers say that about you?

Everywhere you look, best practices are waiting to be discovered. Which company makes buying a pleasure? Nordstrom is devoted to this cause. Where is it enjoyable to test or try a sample? Häagen-Dazs wants you to sample every flavor. Which organizations are great at teaching new customers how to get the most from their products and their service? In Portland, Oregon, Apple buses senior citizens from the local community center to its stores and teaches them to use a computer, some for the very first time. Who delivers most conveniently or quickly? Pizza Hut will have dinner on your doorstep in fewer than 45 minutes. Where is upgrading super simple? Many online software services require no more than a click. Which company is best at bouncing back if you are not completely happy? L.L.Bean makes it guaranteed. Who are the leaders in connecting their customers into a community on Facebook, LinkedIn, Google, or any other forum?

Benchmark Beyond Your Competition

Competitive analysis is worthwhile, but is more likely to promote emulation and fine-tuning than breakthrough innovations. Service Benchmarking invites you to look outside your own industry for ideas outside of the usual box. Become curious about every other industry. Look more closely in all directions. Who creates a great experience face-to-face, in the store, at your home, during delivery, on the web, on the phone, by email, by text, by chat? Who impresses the customers they serve day and night; with comfort and choice; with security, speed, and smiles?

For example, Changi Airport wants you to enjoy personalized, stress-free, and positively surprising service. So the airport installed a lush butterfly garden, which is an incredible place to be personally uplifted, and a twisting, four-story slide that offers unexpected thrills and family excitement. But no other airport in the world provided these as competitive benchmarks. Where did they get these great ideas?

Changi Airport schedules aircraft, allocates specialized aircraft gates, and welcomes visitors who accompany arriving and departing passengers. Hospitals schedule surgeries, allocate specialized operating theaters, and welcome visitors who accompany recovering patients. Hospitals have long used gardens as quiet places to help people rest and relax in a personalized and stress-free environment. And in many of the world's best gardens, you will enjoy the grace and beauty of butterflies.

Changi Airport welcomes families from all over the world with children who have energy to burn and want to enjoy a good time. Theme parks offer engaging attractions and amusing rides to families with children who have energy to burn and want to enjoy a good time. And in many of the world's best theme parks your family will discover multi-story slides.

Let your appetite for improvement inside fuel your curiosity about what's working on the outside. "Who does what we do, but does it better?" is a good question for competitive comparison. The more powerful question for Service Benchmarking is, "Who creates an experience that makes their customers feel the way we want our customers to feel?"

Benchmark the Architecture of Service Culture

You can build an uplifting service culture by benchmarking how others are doing the same. The architecture introduced in section 1 includes Service Leadership, which we discussed in section 2; the 12 Building Blocks of Service Culture, which we are exploring in section 3; and Actionable Service Education, which you will discover in section 4. All of these can be benchmarked.

Service Leadership: Study successful leaders with unyielding commitments to service and the legendary companies they lead: Richard Branson at Virgin, Lou Gerstner, the former CEO at IBM, the Nordstrom family, Walt Disney, L.L.Bean, and Jack Mitchell, the CEO who wrote *Hug Your Customers*. Study their histories, read their biographies, and then follow their lead to the top.

Common Service Language: At Starbucks, employees speak a common language, making it easy for them to coordinate with each other and deliver great service to customers. This is the result of their vigorous efforts to promote and encourage the language. Do your customers understand your language of service as well? Are you doing as much as Starbucks is to teach them?

Engaging Service Vision: Who has a motto, tagline, slogan, or statement that really turns their people on? FedEx employees proudly say their blood runs purple. What do your people say?

Service Recruitment: Zappos sets a standard for selecting team members who *really* want to work there. You can visit their national offices and benchmark them for free. Find out how at Zappos.com.

Service Orientation: The integrated orientation program for all employees based at Changi Airport connects them to the facility, the airlines, the passengers, the nation, and each other. How well does your program help new team members connect?

Service Communications: Political campaigns, sports contests, and celebrity stories are broadcast around the world with repetition and record speed. Your communications may have a different objective, but how can you get the same level of awareness and engagement?

Service Recognition and Rewards: The Nobel Prize, Olympic Gold, and the Hall of Fame. Our global culture is rich with traditions and moments of glory. Is your service culture as abundant? Is "employee of the month" the best that you can do?

Voice of the Customer: Remember the last time someone listened carefully to what you think and feel? When was the last time someone paid close attention to every word you wrote?

These experiences are high on a scale of interest and attention. On that same scale, what do you want your customers to feel when they speak and write to you?

Service Measures and Metrics: Google measures every possible data point to serve you with the best pages, answers, links, and advertising offers. The Japanese word *kaizen* means "continuous improvement and change for the better." Who will you study to make your use of measures even better? How much better can you become with the measures that you use?

Service Improvement Process: Singapore Airlines consistently scores at or near the top of every service ranking and has done so for many years. It's not from having access to better airports, travel websites, or travel agents—or even better aircraft. Every other airline has access to the same. Singapore Airlines' dedication to continuous service improvement is what makes it such a great way to fly. It uses every Service Improvement Process to fine-tune, upgrade, and even transform its customer service. Which do you use as well?

Service Recovery and Guarantees: If anything goes wrong, we promise to make it right. There are lifetime guarantees, money-back guarantees, and 100,000-mile warranties. What promises do your customers deserve? What do your colleagues deserve? Is satisfaction with your service guaranteed?

Service Benchmarking: You can learn how other organizations benchmark by asking these questions: "Where did you learn that?" "Where did you get that idea?" and "How did you make that work so well?" Anytime they do not answer, "We made it up ourselves," you are moving closer to discovering their benchmark.

Service Role Modeling: Watch the waiter who earns the biggest tips. Find out which professor has the highest student rankings.

See which vendor gets the most five-star ratings. Notice the service provider where you work that everyone else looks up to. What is he or she doing that you could do, too? How can you learn from his or her example?

Actionable Service Education: Study companies with integrated suites of top-down and bottom-up service learning. You may have to look hard until this becomes a more common practice. Perhaps you and your organization will see the benchmark in this domain.

Benchmarking Can Be Easy

Traditional business benchmarking is a high-level activity with careful target selection, substantial pre-visit planning, and a rigorous process of post-visit evaluation and implementation. You can do this, too. But don't let a thorough and detailed approach stop you from encouraging a much simpler version of benchmarking. Remember, one of the goals is for everyone to become curious about learning and improving.

Each phone call can be a benchmarking moment. Did the person you were speaking with make you feel appreciated, welcome, confident, or understood? What did he or she say? How did he or she do that? Can you use that in your next call? Each incoming email is one to evaluate and emulate if it moves you to positive action. Each meeting is a possible benchmarking moment, another opportunity to appreciate, adapt, and apply.

An easy way to start benchmarking is to have people inside your organization learn from visiting each other. Is your customer service team known for its friendliness and flexibility? Ask the finance team to make a benchmarking visit. Are your finance team members respected for their accuracy and speed? Ask the delivery team to make a benchmarking visit. Is any one branch, factory, or outlet admired by everyone else? Ask that group to extend an invitation and welcome frequent visits from its peers.

Everyone Can Do Service Benchmarking

When you organize a visit to an outside organization, include people from different levels in your organization. Those who work on the front line may not understand certain details those in higher positions do, but they will see things from a different perspective, often with insights of equal value.

A membership club I frequent features the restaurants, pools, tennis courts, and other facilities you would naturally expect to find. But the Service Benchmarking process is one I have not found anywhere else in the world. During the orientation of new team members, participants are paired up. Each pair is assigned to benchmark one of the nearby five-star hotels where some of the world's highest service standards are on display. They are asked to visit the hotel and to return four hours later, after enjoying a treat in the hotel's coffee shop.

Before the pairs depart, everyone reviews the benchmarking assignment. Each team must discover where the hotel excels and where it could improve:

1. Observe the hotel carefully from the outside. What looks terrific? What needs to be improved?
2. Approach the hotel. How are you greeted?
3. Enter the lobby and walk around. Are you welcomed and offered help?

4. Find the house phone. Ask the operator for a restaurant recommendation. Ask what time the restaurant opens for dinner. Ask what is the soup of the day?

5. Find the lobby shop and ask where you can buy a bouquet of flowers.

6. Go to the coffee shop. Enjoy a drink and a snack while observing carefully every moment of the service.

7. Discuss your experience with your partner. Take notes during your visit when you can.

8. Be ready to share with the group: What was most impressive? What did you find surprising? What could still be improved? What did you learn that could be applied here at our membership club?

Imagine the impact of this visit during someone's first few days on the job, comparing service experiences with some of the best in the world. New employees are asked to explore and think; they are trusted to evaluate, compare, and recommend. This experience itself is a benchmark. How could you adapt and apply it?

Be a Generous Benchmarker

Winners of many national quality awards are asked to showcase their practices for others as a condition of winning the award. This encourages everyone to keep improving.

When you ask another organization for permission to visit and learn, be sure to return the value. Promise to share a report about what you learn, or conduct a presentation showing how you will apply it. Let your "target" know you will help them grow as they help you improve. And when you are ready for the highest levels of Service Benchmarking, invite the recognized leaders to come and benchmark you.

Questions for Service Providers

- What can you learn by studying the service you receive from other people?
- What can you learn by studying the service culture in other organizations?
- Who delivers great service inside your organization? What can you do differently to follow their example?

Questions for Service Leaders

- Who are you benchmarking now? What do you want to learn?
- Who does the benchmarking inside your organization? Who else could you involve in this vital learning process?
- What lessons have you learned from your benchmarking efforts? What actions have you taken to apply these insights?

CHAPTER 18

Service Role Modeling

Why is Service Role Modeling the final building block in an uplifting service culture? Is it less important than the others? Not at all. This is a case of saving the best for last.

Imagine you are developing strength and alignment in each of the other building blocks. Your organization's vision is clear, recruitment is effective, communications, rewards, and measures are all aligned. But your boss doesn't behave as though he believes it. Would you believe it?

Now imagine your organization is improving in the other building blocks, but it's clearly a work in progress. The service language is not yet common, some communications are out-of-date, the recognition program needs fine-tuning, and a service guarantee doesn't even exist. But your manager comes to work each day obviously committed. She walks the talk and makes things happen, fixing problems, resolving issues, and frequently asking for your help. She talks about uplifting service every day and takes action because she believes it. Would you believe it, too?

The Bellman in the Lobby

Jean-Pierre is the general manager of a well-known exclusive hotel in Paris. He is the kind of impeccable gentleman you would expect to see in this position. He knows fine dining and fine wines. He adores the city and admires his upscale guests. He is worldly in his manners and elegant in his appearance.

But four times a year, Jean-Pierre becomes a bellman. One day each quarter he does not enter the building through the luxurious main lobby, as he does on every other day, but rather enters through the staff entrance at the back of the hotel. Like every other member of the staff, he passes through security clearance and then descends to basement level two, where a locker holds his bellman's uniform and cap.

All day, Jean-Pierre greets guests at the roadside, places their bags on a luggage trolley, and escorts them to their rooms. He holds umbrellas in the rain, carries packages in his arms, delivers documents to guests in meetings—and occasionally receives a tip.

The staff members know that Jean-Pierre is really the general manager, but most of his guests do not. Throughout the day he uses this masquerade to seek out real customer comments of great value. "Have you stayed with us before?" he asks a guest. "Is the hotel any better, or worse, since the last time you were here? Where else do you like to stay when you travel? Does any other hotel do things for you that you wish we did, too? How is your room? Is everything up to your expectations? Any messages you'd like me to pass along to the hotel manager?" Guests enjoy this gregarious bellman who seems to love his job, and they share with him candid feedback a general manager might not hear.

At mealtimes, Jean-Pierre takes his lunch and dinner in the staff cafeteria on basement level one. With his bellman's cap sitting on the table, he looks like any other member of the staff. Team members sit with him and talk about their jobs, listen to his questions, and ask questions of their own. He shares ideas and listens to theirs. He cherishes these four days, as do the members of his team. Seeing their general manager in the cafeteria, pushing a luggage trolley through the lobby, or holding an umbrella in the rain, they feel even more proud of him as their leader.

The Coin on the Floor

Sometimes the things we let stand set a negative tone and a poor example for those around us.

Recently I visited the showroom of a European car dealer. I was awed by the automotive engineering, but I was not impressed by the attitude of the staff. Something in the air, a touch of arrogance, that uncomfortable glance from a salesman that warns, "If you have to ask how much it is, you probably can't afford it."

Walking between two of the most expensive cars, I saw a large and shiny coin resting on the floor. The coin looked curious and inviting, but when I stooped down to pick it up, I discovered to my embarrassment that this attractive piece of money had been firmly glued to the floor.

I stood up and sheepishly looked around. The salesmen snickered. The technicians saw it all through the workshop window and they were having a good laugh at my expense. I was certainly not the first customer to be caught by this practical joke.

A coin doesn't get glued to the ground by accident, and doesn't remain there without leadership consent. No wonder there was condescension in the air—it was sanctioned at the top and indulged in on the floor.

Creating Role Models from the Inside Out

Service Role Modeling is not only what you do with customers—it's also what you do and say with the members of your team.

When NTUC Income embarked on a cultural revolution, the new CEO Tan Suee Chieh knew he was asking people to change their traditional way of thinking and their comfortable way of being. The best thing he could do was model new behaviors for all to see and follow.

He wanted his people to be more flexible, so Mr. Tan took up intensive yoga classes to demonstrate his commitment to be flexible and balanced. He wanted the team to think and act outside their comfort zones, so he shaved his head for a charity function and proudly displayed the results. He wanted the team to use new media, go online, and not be afraid of the digital future. So he created a Twitter account, Facebook pages, and a LinkedIn profile to connect himself and his company to the world.

Now he wants the company to be fit for the competitive future and is training to run a full marathon. Some in the company will join him on the run. And, through his behavior, everyone will be uplifted by his commitment.

Your team members notice every consistency and every contradiction. You can't ask your team to respond quickly to customers if your own meetings do not start on time. You can't ask for great organization and housekeeping if your own office is a mess. You can't ask your people to be polite and gracious if you swear with impunity behind closed doors. You can't ask your team members to provide uplifting service if you don't serve them with passion as an uplifting service leader.

Being a Role Model at Every Level

Being a service role model is not just for senior managers and members of the leadership team. It is what happens every time people can see what you do, read what you write, or hear what you say in an internal or external service situation.

Being a role model is present in your tone of voice when speaking to a vendor. It's the way you respond to a customer in a difficult situation. It's how you phrase a written message when you choose to disagree. Being a role model is how you participate on a team, set the mood in an awkward situation, or take the lead with your clear commitment to a purpose or a project. Being a role model is exhibited in every action you take that demonstrates your attitude, skills, and behavior—and not only when other people are listening or watching. What you do when no one else can see you is being a model for yourself.

Chasing a Role Model in the Sky

"How many restaurants are up here?" Todd Nordstrom asked Matthew Daines, an executive at Marina Bay Sands who was leading us on a tour of the stunning SkyPark—57 stories above the bustling city of Singapore.

"Well, there's . . ." began Mr. Daines, before he instantly bolted away and ran ahead of us.

"Where's he going?" asked Todd, watching Mr. Daines sprint along the side of the infinity pool, swoop up a camera left on a bench, and continue dodging through visitors as he ran. Todd chuckled. "Wow, he's got some quick feet. Zigzagging through the crowd in a full suit."

"Oh, I see. That woman he's chasing must have left her camera on the bench," I said as we trailed behind. "He really is moving."

Todd and I caught up with Mr. Daines on the observation deck as the guest was thanking him for returning her camera. He was smiling politely, and was a bit out of breath.

"Ma'am," he called out as she began walking away. "Since we're up here, would you like me to take your picture?"

The woman smiled with delight. "We'd love that. You are too kind."

I nudged Todd as Mr. Daines snapped pictures of the woman and her friend who were clearly excited to have their picture taken together. Off to the side were two restaurant servers. Behind us was a maintenance team member, and around us were other guests who had seen the whole incident unfold.

"Look who's watching," I said. "See all their smiles? Can you guess what they are thinking?"

Questions for Service Providers

- What can you do in your organization today to set the tone and the pace for uplifting service?
- How can you and your colleagues take the lead as positive service role models?

Questions for Service Leaders

- When was the last time you did something that caused your team members to say, "Wow! Our leader really believes in uplifting service!"?
- What else can you do to be a role model for your customers, colleagues, company, industry, and for society?
- What is your "coin on the floor"? What are your behaviors that send the wrong service signal to your staff?

SECTION FOUR

LEARN

CHAPTER 19

Learning Takes Practice

As the lights dim, the audience quiets to a whisper. A spotlight travels across the small wooden stage to a microphone standing in the middle. Suddenly a tall man bursts out from behind the curtain waving at the eager audience and shouting "Is everyone ready for a great time tonight?"

The crowd goes wild.

This was open microphone night at a small comedy club in midtown New York City. And it was Roger Staples' first attempt at stand-up comedy.

Roger had grown up in the midwestern United States. Now, in his mid-20s, he worked as part-time disc jockey. But he had always dreamed of being a comedian. He studied all the famous American comedians—spending his free time watching their shows and listening to recordings while he drove. He even read the transcripts of their shows. Roger studied every book he could find about comedy and laughter. He knew the complete history of humorists from jesters to modern-day comics. He knew the difference between satire, slapstick, and stand-up, and could explain what makes people laugh and giggle.

But Roger also knew that just reading and writing jokes wasn't enough—he also had to impress people with his confidence and charisma on the stage. So he read every book he could find on public speaking and presentations to prepare for his first show. He read, and read, and read.

Yet, that night, when Roger stepped in front of the microphone, he looked out at the smiling audience, and his mind went blank. His jaw locked. And after 41 brutal seconds of silence, Roger walked off stage without saying a word.

Why? What happened?

Although Roger had studied every book, he never actually *learned* the art of stand-up comedy. He could talk about it, but he couldn't do it. All he knew was in his head, but it wasn't in his body. It's like reading every weight loss book but not exercising or changing your diet. Or like watching a movie about riding a bicycle without getting on—and falling off—to learn pedaling, steering, and balance.

The same is true with service. It's not enough to only read this book and know the language of uplifting service—you must apply the practices, too. There are four approaches people and organizations can take when it comes to learning about uplifting service. Which category best describes your team or your organization? Which category best describes you?

The Do Nothings: People in this group do absolutely nothing to elevate their service levels or boost their employees' understanding of service. They continue day after day as if service improvement is irrelevant, unimportant, or simply someone else's job.

The Lip Servers: The lip servers say they will provide good service in marketing messages, and encourage it with motivating posters on the wall, but they don't provide any tools for learning or improvement. It's basically an empty message communicated by leadership that becomes an empty promise to customers and just noise to employees.

The Process Trainers: Process trainers spend time and money on customer service training, and then wonder why no substantial improvements are made or why enthusiasm stalls shortly after. This is the vital difference between training and service education. Training teaches people how to do something: take specific actions in specific situations, use a script, follow a checklist, or complete a procedure. Training is essential when the service provider must do just the right thing at exactly the right moment. Pilots and surgeons, for example, are carefully trained to follow procedures and are regularly checked on their skills.

But training is tactical and prescriptive and will often differ among functions. In a large service organization, this leads to a fragmented understanding of what service means to different colleagues, and for different customers. Process training often leaves employees uncertain what to do in situations they have not been trained to handle. And since customers' needs and interests are always changing, this leads to frequent escalations that consume managers' time, and leaves frontline staff members feeling disengaged and disempowered.

The Service Educators: Service educators are different. They engage every member of the team in an ongoing learning adventure. They know that becoming skillful in service does not happen all at once, just as mastering math or learning a new language cannot be accomplished in a single session. If you are in this group, you know that service education must be frequent, repeated, reviewed, and renewed for everyone on a continuous and uplifting basis.

Training teaches someone what actions to take in a specific situation. Education teaches him or her how to think about service in any situation and then choose the best actions to take. Service educators teach fundamental service principles. They develop relevant case studies, customized exercises, challenging simulations, and practical discussions with key learning points to apply. They teach with real-time data, current customer comments, compliments, complaints, and competitive information. And the service educators don't stop there. They insist that service education must lead to practical action steps for each person and position. And it must be valuable for every colleague and customer served.

If you are a service educator, you know that new learning happens when principles are put into action, new insights are discovered, new skills are developed, and new understanding and competencies are secured. Just reading a book won't uplift your service performance or build your service culture. This is why the chapters in this book include so many action steps. It takes new action to uplift your service and delight the people around you.

Finally, service educators use methods of teaching that are uplifting. Service skills and attitudes are delivered and experienced together. Manufacturing requires a competent skillset. Service requires a competent successful skillset *and* an uplifting service mindset.

Education Can Be Exciting

"Pretty amazing, isn't it?" I asked Todd Nordstrom as we stood at the curb waiting for a taxi outside Marina Bay Sands. "Everyone in this property gets it."

Todd nodded as he continued to snap photos with his phone.

"Mr. Kaufman!" someone screamed from the distance. "Mr. Ron Kaufman!" Todd stopped taking pictures. "Who's that?" he asked as a man ran toward us.

"Mr. Ron, welcome back!" the man said with a gleeful smile. "Let me get a taxi for you."

The man put his fingers to his lips and whistled while waving his other arm in the air. Todd watched him with curiosity. And, he listened carefully as the nice man and I exchanged greetings.

As soon as the taxi doors closed, Todd turned his head back to see the man waving good-bye. "A friend of yours?" he asked.

"I met him a few weeks ago when I came here for a luncheon," I responded. "He's a great guy. He really understands. That's the level of enthusiasm every company wishes it could get from its employees when they deliver service."

"No kidding," said Todd. "Any hotel would be thrilled to hire an upbeat guy like that."

"Yes," I said. "But that level of enthusiasm isn't just good recruiting. Marina Bay Sands continuously educates its team members so they provide that level of service in all kinds of situations."

"You can't train someone to get that excited," said Todd.

"No, you can't," I said, agreeing. "But you can educate them, and they will get themselves that excited to serve."

CHAPTER 20

The Six Levels of Service

Yanti Karmasanto was shopping in her hometown of Jakarta, Indonesia, after lunch. She wandered into one of the large shopping malls that had popped up where a farm had stood when she was young. Music poured from every shop in an unpredictable medley of tunes. As Yanti passed one storefront, the music inside suddenly stopped and the shopkeeper let out a growl. She looked inside and saw something most of us have not seen for years, if ever. The shopkeeper had been changing the music in his boom box. As he pulled out an old cassette, all the thin metallic tape spilled out in a dusty mess on the floor.

Do you remember that? Are you old enough to remember phonograph records that could be accidentally scratched? Or eight-track tapes? Cracked CDs? Do you remember when you had to go downtown to buy new music, before you could simply download it to your phone or computer? Today, music is skip-free, scratch-free, and never gathers dust.

Of course, it's easy to see how technology is constantly changing throughout our lives. Companies that manufacture products understand that they must always be introducing something new, faster, easier, or better to keep their customers engaged. If they don't, they will be left in the dust when their customers upgrade to the next new product.

But very few companies understand that service is exactly the same—it's always changing, and it's your job to stay ahead of your customers, ahead of the competition, and ahead of the curve. Service is not about what you do, the

processes you use, or how well you follow procedures. Service is about the experience and the value you create for someone else.

Let's start by figuring out your current level of service. Whether you serve external customers or internal colleagues, your service will fit into one of the Six Levels of Service. Consider your level of service from someone else's point of view. Is your service:

Criminal: Criminal-level service breaks a service promise; it violates even minimum expectations. Customers remember to never use a company with this kind of service again, and are sometimes angry enough to contact you and complain about it. And if they don't tell you, they will very likely tell others. This kind of bad-news service gets plenty of airtime and can go viral online in an instant.

Basic: Basic service is disappointing; it's the bare minimum. This level of service leads to frustration—it's late, slow, incomplete, or impolite. But when it's over, thank goodness it's over. And your customer may not complain. However, he or she may well tell friends to avoid your company, and will certainly remember not to come back for that kind of service again.

Expected: Expected service is nothing special. Your customer might come back to you, but only if there are no better options. This level of industry-standard service used to be considered acceptable. After all, the outdated definition of customer satisfaction was simply "meeting expectations." But in today's world, that level doesn't win any loyalty.

Desired: Desired service is what other people hope for and prefer. This level describes service that is delivered just the way another person likes it. For one person, this could be extra fast, flexible, or friendly. For another, it might be very personal, or it might involve a range of prices, packages, or options. Desired service brings people back; it gives them what they value in the manner they desire.

Surprising: Surprising service is something special, like an unexpected gift. Surprising gives your customers more than they expected, making you an individual or an organization that attracts a following and stands out from the crowd. Customers come to surprising service providers again and again, and they are glad to tell their friends. But delivering this surprising level of service is not just a matter of enthusiasm and excitement. You must actually understand what the person you are serving really values.

Has anyone ever given you a gift you truly enjoyed—one that you were genuinely surprised and delighted by? Remember how good it felt? And has anyone ever given you a gift that was not such a wonderful surprise, but instead it actually created an awkward moment? Maybe they gave you something *they* valued and were sure that you would love it. Or they gave you something you *used* to value, but your tastes and interests had moved on.

What is the difference between these two situations? In both cases, someone else chose, bought, wrapped, and presented you with a gift they intended as a nice surprise. In one case, the person succeeded. In the other case, the person failed. The difference was not in their intentions; it was in their understanding of your needs and desires. Surprising service does not mean enthusiastic leaps of joy from excited service providers— unless that is what your customers or colleagues want and value. Surprising service means knowing what another person appreciates and values most, and then giving them more than he or she expected.

Unbelievable: Unbelievable service is astonishing and fantastic. This level of service people never forget. These experiences may even become legendary, fondly shared by loyal customers and talked about with pride by colleagues. These are acts of deeply passionate service providers and organizations that pride themselves on delivery of extraordinary service.

One home security alarm company in New Zealand prides itself on ABCD Service: Above and Beyond the Call of Duty. Whenever these teams visit homeowners for installations, system checks, or upgrades, they will not leave the home until they have done two extra tasks that help the homeowner but have nothing to do with the security system. They might fix a leaky faucet, oil a squeaky hinge, or help repair a broken chair or window. These extra service moments have nothing to do with the efficiency of the 24-hour home security system, but everything to do with this company's strong commercial success and *unbelievable* service reputation.

Six Levels of Internal Service

These Six Levels of Service help you see the world from your customer's point of view. They apply to every person in every position and in every moment of service, including when you and your colleagues serve each other.

Suppose you ask a colleague for help and he ignores your request. So you ask again, but he says, "I'm really busy." You need his help to answer a customer's question, so you reach out one more time. He gives you something so you will go away, but the information is wrong and now your customer is distressed. That's a criminal level of internal service. Suppose you ask another colleague for help to finish a project. She does what you ask, but does it late and incompletely. So you have to go back to ask a second time to get what was missing. That's not a good experience, but eventually you get what you need. It's a basic level of service. When you ask a colleague for help and he gives you what you need on time, that's normal in most business situations. It's expected.

Now let's explore the higher levels. Imagine a co-worker gives you the information you need quickly and with a smile. And then he says, "If you need anything else, just ask. I'll be glad to assist you." In most working relationships, this would be desired. Taking this one step further, suppose he answers your questions and provides a bit of extra information that is relevant to your request. You didn't ask for this, but what he tells you makes your work easier and more successful. Your colleague's extra effort is unexpected and appreciated. It's surprising.

Finally, imagine your colleague tells his department colleagues about your request and they all decide to help you get the job done, faster, more completely, and better than ever before. That's an unprecedented level of internal service. It's unbelievable.

The Stairs Are Always Sliding Down

The big challenge with these Six Levels of Service is not discovering where you are—you can find that out by asking honestly and listening carefully to those you serve. The real test will come because the stairs themselves are not fixed; they are always moving like an escalator—going down. What starts out as surprising soon becomes desired. And after a while, it's just expected, or even basic. Then, before you know it, everyone is wondering what's new.

The escalator of service standards is accelerated by competition. Other service providers are always looking for new ways to climb to the next level, to create an even better customer experience. As a result, customer expectations are constantly rising. Standing still becomes slipping down when your competitors are moving up. Even doing what's expected is no longer satisfactory to succeed. This sliding escalator phenomenon makes service excellence a moving target. There is only one way to be consistently excellent in service—you must always be stepping up.

When a company reaches the top of its field, staying there means stepping up more than ever. At the Singapore Airlines Cabin Crew Training Centre, one visitor from Korea asked in admiration, "How does Singapore Airlines stay on top all these years? And how do you plan to keep the lead while other airlines work so hard to beat you?"

Mr. Sim Kay Wee, former Senior Vice President of Cabin Crew, answered clearly: "One hundred percent is not enough. When you reach number one, you need 120 percent. And here's why: If you fly on a mediocre airline, your service expectation may be only 50 percent. If the cabin crew is in a good mood, they may actually deliver 65 percent. Then what is your opinion of the service? It's up 15 percent.

"But if you know Singapore Airlines is number one," he continued, "what is your expectation of the service? Maybe 110 percent. If our cabin crew delivers service at the 100 percent level, then what is your opinion of our service? It's down 10 percent!

"This is the challenge of being number one," Mr. Sim concluded. "If you are in the lead and want to stay there, 100 percent is not enough. You need every member of the team to keep stepping up even higher."

Stepping up or slipping down happens inside organizations, too. If one department steps up to a higher level of internal service and the other departments don't follow, then by comparison the other departments are slipping down. If you make a personal service improvement in your service attitude or skills, then you have stepped up another level. By comparison, if the people you work with just keep doing the same old thing, then by default they would be seen as slipping down. Promotions are earned by stepping up at work every day. Strong partnerships are created when everyone steps up together.

What Level of Service Should You Provide?

What level of service should you seek to deliver on a daily basis? Avoiding criminal and basic levels should be obvious, because these will degrade your service reputation, driving away good customers and colleagues. Delivering expected service may be adequate, but it's just one step away from basic. Providing desired service means giving people what they want, the way they want. That's an admirable and achievable standard you should aim for every day.

When should you go beyond expectations and give surprising service, or even stretch to unbelievable? First, whenever you want to create a long-lasting impression and a powerful service memory. Second, when you want to demonstrate your ability to blow away the competition or positively blow your customers' minds. Third, when you are bouncing back after something has gone wrong, providing a surprising service experience is a good recovery technique. And finally, whenever you see an opportunity to give spectacular levels of service without increasing your costs or hassles, then by all means do it. Chances are your competition will discover the same opportunity moments later, but you will get there first. Every moment can become a positive moment when you step up to provide a higher level of service. The only question that matters is this: Will you lead, or will you follow?

Questions for Service Providers

- This week, keep track of the service you receive. What delights you? What disappoints you? Notice how each service provider uses, or loses, the opportunity to give you a higher level of quality service.
- How can you acknowledge the people who give you uplifting service? Can you write a compliment? Post a nice online review? Leave a tip, or share an extra smile?

Questions for Service Leaders

- Can all your team members explain why stepping up their service makes good business sense? Can you explain so each team member is inspired to take new action?
- Which customers can you invite into a meeting with your team? What questions will you ask so they will candidly tell you about your service?

CHAPTER 21

Your Perception Points

Keri Childers did not like this situation. Her all-in-one office printer, scanner, and fax machine had stopped working. It was a big machine that stood on the floor. It was still under on-site warranty, so a technician would be coming into her home office to provide the necessary repair. Someone she didn't know. The doorbell rang and the service technician presented himself, his company ID, and the service repair order. So she let him inside, and that's when the unexpected happened.

When she led him to the faulty device, he put down his bag full of tools and then pulled out a white pair of gloves and put them on. To her surprise, he asked, "Before I get started, may I move some of these other things out of the way? I wouldn't want to knock them over accidentally while I work." She smiled as he carefully moved away a standing lamp, two framed photographs, and a neatly organized stack of books.

Then he reached into his bag, took out a small blanket, and laid it ceremoniously in front of the machine. "I don't want to scratch or stain your floor," he said. Then he opened the machine, took out his tools, and diligently went to work. Thirty minutes later, when the repair was done and tested, Keri signed the paperwork and thanked him very much.

"Sure thing." He smiled. "We are glad to be of service." And then he reached into his bag and pulled out yet another unexpected item: a small spray can of lemon-scented furniture polish. "Would you mind if I touch it up before I go?" he asked. Keri nodded and watched in surprise as he lightly sprayed the front and sides of the machine, rubbed them down with a cloth, and put everything back in his bag. Then he put the white gloves on again and moved her lamp, photographs, and stack of books right back in place.

After the technician left, Keri's office was filled with the pleasant lemon fragrance. One of her children bounded around the corner and asked, "What's that nice smell, Mommy?" Keri answered, still smiling to herself with some amazement, "It was from the repairman, honey. And what a nice surprise."

Service Is Delivered in a Sequence

All service is delivered in a sequence, a natural series of moments that include a beginning, middle, and end. For example, buying a new office device is a transaction involving shopping, comparing, possibly negotiating, eventually deciding, ordering, and making payment. Having the new device installed is a related but different transaction. This one involves scheduling; unpacking; installing; loading software, paper, and cartridges; testing; and, finally, confirming the whole thing works. A repair call is yet another transaction, also with multiple points of service along the way.

Each sequence of service you deliver is called a Service Transaction. The moments when people experience your service and form their opinions are called Perception Points. All of these Perception Points are evaluated—consciously or unconsciously—on the Six Levels of Service. Some may be very pleasant and surprising, as Keri discovered. Others could be so usual or expected that you hardly even notice. And some points could be disappointing. How many Perception Points must fall below expected to damage your service reputation?

The honest and frightening answer is—just one.

Suppose you read a good review about a new restaurant on a website—that's a positive first Perception Point. But when you call to make a dinner reservation, the individual answering the phone is not cheerful or helpful. So you make a decision to go somewhere else. And here's the disturbing insight. All the other people who work at the restaurant and need customers to make a living don't even know this problem happened. Just one disappointing moment delivered by one of many employees—waiter, chef, hostess, manager, dishwasher, and busboy—destroyed the dinner reservation.

On the other hand, how many Perception Points need to be surprising to make your dinner a special treat? Again, the answer is just one. And that's good news! If everything else is as expected, but the music is delightful, or the dessert is something special, or your waiter is terrific, any one of these can make your evening special, and inspire you to want to come back.

What does this mean for every organization and every service team? What does this mean for you and your colleagues? Each person is counting on others to deliver their Perception Points of service *at least* at the expected level. But because the stairs are always slipping down, each person must also be actively seeking to take the next step up. In a culture of uplifting service, this is exactly what you and your colleagues will be doing every day.

Mapping Your Perception Points

You can map the Perception Points in each Service Transaction you deliver. Chart them in a circle from start to finish. Mapping your Perception Points is not the same as charting the processes you use—your service systems, tools, and procedures. Rather, Perception Points are the individual points where customers form their opinions about the service you provide and the experience you deliver.

Perception Points can be mapped in every transaction with your external customers and with your internal colleagues. For the external view, consider your customers' experience when they are interacting with the different parts of your organization. For the internal view consider your colleagues' experience when they are interacting with you.

Service Transactions and Perception Points

Perception Points at the beginning of a transaction form vital first impressions—the ones you never get a second chance to make, or recover. Perception Points toward the end shape lasting final impressions. And all the Perception Points in the middle, of course, connect the two. Many organizations don't appreciate the number of Perception

Points that can be identified, studied, and improved. Remember, it just takes one low point to spoil an interaction and one nice moment of surprise to make the experience memorable.

You can study your Perception Points in sequence, by theme, by category, and even with your senses. And each point of view can be helpful to find new ways of stepping up. First let's explore your Perception Points from a thematic point of view:

Your People: What opinions are formed by your team members' professionalism, personality, dress code, eye contact, body language, voice tone, vocabulary and pronunciation, product knowledge, process knowledge, punctuality, flexibility, and level of confidence in your organization, their colleagues, and themselves?

Your Product: Every point about your product shapes and forms opinion. What perception do customers have of your product's features, performance, design, durability, ease of operation and maintenance, availability, compatibility, upgradability, power consumption, and price?

Your Packaging: In some cases and cultures, packaging is as influential as what is inside the package. Is yours well-designed, functional, and attractive? Is it recyclable, reusable, or disposable? Whether presenting a meal, a carton, a contract, a gift, or a proposal, your packaging may be as important as the content.

Your Place: If your place of business has a physical location, is it well located and well lit, with good signage, convenient hours, and easy access for differently abled people? If your place of business is online, is your site easy to navigate, fast to load, attractive, pleasantly interactive, secure, and up-to-date? If you do business at your customer's location, are your vehicles well marked and your people well attired?

Your Promotions: Marketing shapes the public's perceptions and expectations of your service. Is your offer compelling? Is your advertising attractive? Do the public faces of your organization project the service image you desire?

Your Policies: Do your customers feel welcomed, tolerated, or punished by your policies for pricing, payment, warranty, guarantee, maintenance, delivery and returns? Are your policies sensible and easy for customers to understand? Do they make doing business with you a pleasure or a pain? Do they make you appear trusting and trustworthy, or cynical and selfish?

Your Processes: Is your service fast? Do your lines run long? Are you speedy or slow in responding to questions and requests? Is your process one-stop, one-click, or a single point of contact? Do you handle all the details, or ask your customers to do the work? If your process includes using the telephone, how long do customers wait on hold? Are your employees' voices warm and friendly? Are messages taken clearly? Does anyone ever call back? Can your people solve a problem on the spot?

Exploring with Your Senses

People use all their senses when forming opinions about your service, as Keri and one of her children discovered with surprise. You can use this to improve your service in many ways.

What do people see? Review the photos, fonts, and colors on your website. Create an email signature that projects a positive image. Update old items hanging on the walls. Throw out whatever is no longer current. Replace every light bulb that isn't working. Scrub the handrails and sweep the sidewalks. Cut away dead leaves on your office plants. Put on a fresh coat of paint. Get a haircut. Shine your shoes. Clean and press your clothing. Look around again with fresh and curious eyes. What else can you do to polish your Perception Points and improve your visual image?

What do people hear? What voices, words, tones, tunes, and volumes do your customers hear at each Perception Point? Is the background noise a pleasure or distraction? Is your voice mail message engaging and up-to-date? Give yourself an auditory audit and you will hear many opportunities to improve. And put a smile on your face when you are speaking—we can't see it over the phone, but we can hear it in your voice.

What do people feel? People feel everything that comes in contact with their clothing or their skin. This includes the weight and texture of everything they touch and handle: the comfort of your chairs, the softness of your carpets, the temperature in your office, the texture of your products, and the smooth or sticky surface of your counters. Touch includes the handshake to connect, the high five to celebrate, and the warm hug to welcome someone back.

What do people taste? Even if you're not in the food and beverage business, people form sweet or sour perceptions about the service you provide. Is there a pantry or a restaurant on-site? Are there snacks or breath mints in the conference room or on the counter? Lick your lips and ponder this: How sweet is the flavor of your service?

What do people smell? Your customers notice fragrances and flowers, breath mints and body odor, mealtimes and machines, production gases and car fumes, and much more. Real estate agents put freshly baked cookies in the kitchen to help sell houses. Smart service providers brush their teeth after every snack and meal. Close your eyes and take a deep breath first thing in the morning, after lunch, and once again at the end of the day. Is the smell of your service environment consistently attractive and appealing?

A Surprising Taste of Service

At Changi Airport, the Service Transaction called "passenger arrival" begins when an aircraft door opens and ends when the taxi door closes. Mapping this Service Transaction identifies many Perception Points: the aerobridge (Is it clean, dry, air-conditioned, and well lit?); the transit area (Are luggage carts available? Is the signage clear?); the immigration counter (Is the line moving quickly?); the baggage belt (How long before the bags arrive?); the duty-free shop (Is it open, well stocked, and well staffed?); the customs officers (Are they helpful and respectful of your belongings?); the arrivals area (Is it crowded and noisy, or clean and clear? Is there a long line to get a taxi?). That's a lot of Perception Points, and Changi Airport studies every one.

One of the airport's ambitions is to be rated the friendliest in the world. But one Perception Point persistently scored low in the "friendly" category on passenger surveys: the immigration counter. Of course, it's not Immigration's primary function to be friendly as much as it is to monitor and manage who enters and leaves the country. But because Changi Airport wants to step up their passengers' experience at every Perception Point, they studied this point carefully and found a new solution. Instead of asking Immigration officers to make friendly small talk with arriving and departing passengers which could distract them from their essential responsibility, slow down the process, and lead to longer waiting times, Changi Airport placed an attractive box of breath mints on each and every counter. Every day, as thousands of passengers hand across their passports for review, Singapore's Immigration officers smile, gesture toward the box, and kindly say one word, "Sweet?" And what was the result of this inexpensive innovation? Immigration's "friendly" scores went up.

Clear, Kept Promises

In a world where the escalator is always slipping down and competition is stepping up, there will be times your Perception Points may fall below some customers' expectations. But this doesn't mean that you—or they—need to suffer. You can be proactive to anticipate their experience and to manage their service expectations.

The long-term approach to managing expectations is a strategy, not a tactic. It takes time to work effectively; you must start it long before you need it. The strategy is "Clear, Kept Promises," and it works exactly as it sounds. You make a clear service promise, and you keep it. You make another clear promise, and you keep it again. Do this over and over again when you serve your customers and your colleagues. In time, you will build a reputation for reliability and a reservoir of goodwill. Once that reservoir is in place, you can call upon it if and when you need it. Should you find yourself temporarily unable to provide your normally uplifting service, all you need to do is apologize and explain the situation. Those you serve will be remarkably understanding—they have an investment in that reservoir of goodwill with you, too.

This strategy only works when you keep the promises you make and when you make your promises crystal clear. There's a big difference between "Don't worry, it's guaranteed," and "This three-year guarantee covers all parts and labor at our service center. On-site service is available for a small extra charge." Dissatisfaction is lurking if you say, "We can process your request within a day," but what you really mean is, "We can process your request within one day once we have your completed application with all supporting documents." And your professionalism is at stake when you say to a colleague, "I'll get this done as soon as I can" instead of "I can complete this for you by four o'clock tomorrow afternoon. Will that be soon enough?"

Clear, Kept Promises also means communicating clearly and quickly when you cannot keep a promise, not waiting for a last-minute leap of effort or a stroke of very good luck to save the day. Sometimes things happen and you cannot deliver what you promised. Should you wait until other people notice (if they notice) and then explain what happened? Should you wait until the very last minute to see what happens? After all, why worry someone else if there may be nothing to worry about?

Let's take a closer look. Suppose you promise to deliver 100 important items to your customer next Thursday. But on Monday morning you discover only 50 left in stock. Your factory says they may get you another 50 just in time, but due to scheduling and weather, it's not a sure thing.

Should you tell your customer as soon as you know that you might not deliver 100? Should you risk creating anxiety and concern when you still have four days to solve the problem? The answer to this question is "Yes." With four days advance notice, your customer will have time to develop a plan. If you wait until Thursday to tell them, it will be impossible for them to prepare. And then if the factory does deliver all the items in time, you will appear as a trustworthy service provider who successfully solved the problem.

When something goes wrong, let other people know as soon as you do. Clear, Kept Promises means communicating early, doing what's needed to take care of those affected, and then making a new service promise. This may seem uncomfortable, but it's your best step forward to build credibility as a trustworthy service partner.

Everyone gets confused at times in the busy turmoil of life. But the people you serve should never be confused about their expectations of service from you. It's a long-term strategy to build goodwill with every promise you keep. Make clear promises and keep them. Communicate early when you can't.

Winning from the Beginning

The second approach to managing expectations is not a strategy; it's a tactic. It is short-term and cannot be applied in every situation. This tactic is called "Under Promise, Over Deliver" and, when used correctly, it will create new opportunities for surprising and uplifting pleasure.

Suppose you are in a store and the salesperson needs to go somewhere else to retrieve the item you ordered. She says, "It will take about five minutes," but she comes back in eight minutes. Are you happy? No. In fact, for the last few minutes you would be looking at your watch and wondering, "Where did she go?"

If a salesperson knows that it's going to take about eight minutes, what should she tell you? "I'll be back in about ten minutes." If she says that, and then she comes back in eight minutes, will you be happy? Yes. And you might even be impressed and say to her, "Wow! You sure are fast!"

So what is the difference between these two situations? Changing just one word from "eight" to "ten." One word and a salesperson's thoughtful use of a proven tactic for managing expectations: Under Promise, Over Deliver.

Time and speed are not the only Perception Points of service during which you can manage expectations. You can do the same with product features, availability, performance, and price. Imagine you work in an electronics store. Someone comes in to buy a camera, looks at and holds different brands, and then chooses a model he likes. Suppose the camera he chooses comes with a carrying case at no extra charge. If you are certain your customer is going to buy this camera, consider telling him about the carrying case *after* he completes the purchase. Then you can smile and say, "Congratulations! Your new camera also comes with this attractive carrying case. And it's free!"

Your customer will feel terrific! He's been given a nice surprise, something extra, something *more* than he expected.

This Under Promise, Over Deliver tactic is not intended to hurt or undermine those you serve. You are managing expectations to influence what others expect, so the service you provide at key Perception Points will satisfy and please them. You win, your colleagues win, and your customers win, too.

Warning: Under Promise, Over Deliver is a short-term tactic, not a long-term strategy. Don't use this with the same person again and again, or the surprising part won't work. And sometimes, it's simply not appropriate. For example, if your competition is promising high and delivering high, then don't promise low. The tactic won't work. If you are pushing for a promotion and your boss has sky-high standards, then promise high performance and deliver even higher.

Questions for Service Providers

- Pretend you are someone who is being served by you. Follow the person's experience from the very start to the finish. How many Perception Points can you see, hear, touch, smell, and taste throughout the process?
- Which of your Perception Points are lowest on the Six Levels of Service in your Service Transactions? What can you do now to step them up?

Questions for Service Leaders

- What are the Service Transactions your team is responsible to deliver? How many Perception Points can you identify and improve?
- Which Perception Points are frequently cited in your customers' complaints? What can you do to improve your customers' experience?
- How can you start winning from the beginning? When is it appropriate for you to manage your customers' and colleagues' expectations?

CHAPTER 22

The BIG Picture

Why is Amazon successful? Why are its sales hitting record numbers with market share rising and customer satisfaction scores climbing every year? Is Amazon successful because it was first to market? Is it because it offers so many books in different formats? Or is it because it now sells so much more than books?

Or is Amazon successful because it is available for you to shop at your convenience anytime from the comfort of your home, your laptop, or your phone? Is it because you can order instantly with its patented "1-Click," or because it will deliver in a week, overnight if you prefer, or allow you to download a digital version right now?

Maybe Amazon is successful because it is service-minded, even if you never see their employees in person or speak to them on the phone. Try returning an item you bought, or sorting out a billing issue. The written messages you receive will be helpful, often personalized, and always friendly.

Or maybe Amazon is successful because it remembers so many things about you, recommending new things for you to read, review, or consider. It knows what you browsed, what you bought, what credit cards you use, the people on your gift list, the reminders you need, and even the gift you sent on Mother's Day last year.

Amazon is successful because the answer to all these questions is "Yes!" Amazon knows that service means creating value. And it understands that different people value different things. Amazon is not just selling useful products; it is providing a powerful service *experience* loaded with customer-pleasing *value.*

Customers shop at Amazon for the products, the low prices, the speed, the convenience, the friendly service, the comfort of what Amazon remembers, and the pleasure of what it recommends. Customers come back to Amazon in increasing numbers for the *surprising experience* of all these areas combined. Amazon consistently delivers, and its many customers appreciate "The BIG Picture."

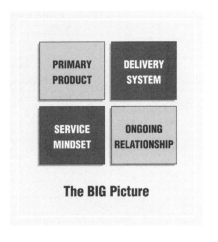

The BIG Picture

You can become a better and more-valued service provider by improving the experience you provide in the same four categories of The BIG Picture: your primary product, your delivery systems, your service mindset, and your ongoing relationship.

Your Primary Product

Everyone is a service provider to someone else. Your Primary Product is the main reason people come to you for service. Why

226

do people come to you in the first place? What is the Primary Product you provide?

In a retail store, Primary Products are easy to see on the website or on the shelf. In a factory, Primary Product is found in the quality of raw materials or the craftsmanship and design. At a restaurant, the Primary Product is food and drink. For a technology developer, Primary Product includes form, function, and features. In a bank, it's minimum balance, annual fees, interest rates, and other terms. For a doctor, it's the accuracy of diagnosis and treatment. The Primary Product for a government agency is useful policies and regulations. Primary Products are very important, which is why they are called primary. But in almost every case, Primary Products can be easily copied.

Internal service providers also deliver important Primary Products to their colleagues. The finance group manages budgets, payments, and collections. The legal team creates contracts and agreements. The human resource department handles recruitment, compensation, and career development. The information technology team keeps your computer systems up and running. These essential internal services are the Primary Products of these departments.

Whatever you serve or sell, create or produce, design, develop, or deliver, your primary product will be seen as stepping up—or sliding down—the Six Levels of Service. Consider your own experiences when trying a new product. Have you ever been delighted by great quality and surprising features? Have you been disappointed by bad workmanship or poor performance? Price is also a feature of the Primary Product. Have you ever enjoyed a package price with an unexpected bonus? Have you been sold a "special bargain" that ended up costing you a great deal more?

What level of quality and what amount of value do you provide with your Primary Products? You don't have to be the biggest or the most expensive to be successful. But you do have to offer what someone else will pay for. How can you create more value in this essential category? You can provide a better product, a wider range of choices, a better package, or more attractive price. As an individual service provider, you can learn and share a wider range of product knowledge.

Your Delivery Systems

Delivery Systems are the processes, methods, and tools you use to get your Primary Products to those you serve. It helps them make a choice, confirm and track their orders, deliver and install the items, invoice and collect the payments, and manage any need that may arise for returns, replacement, repair, or refund. High-value Delivery Systems provide convenience, speed, flexibility, easy choice, and easy access.

In a retail store, Delivery Systems include websites, store locations, opening hours, display of goods, and speed and ease of checkout. In a factory, Delivery Systems include production scheduling, order processing, pallets, containers, warehouses, and trucks. For technology developers, Delivery Systems may include distributors, value-added resellers, retail outlets, online stores, and direct download to your devices. At a bank, Delivery Systems are changing every day: branch locations, ATM networks, online payments, and mobile touch-and-go. With doctors, Delivery Systems include clinics, hospitals, bedside house calls (common in the past), and virtual visits (likely to be more prominent in the future). The Delivery System used by a government agency may be in the office or in the field, over the counter, the web, and on the phone. At a restaurant, Delivery Systems include menus, counters, buffet lines, drive-throughs, pick-ups, and home delivery.

Internal service providers also use a wide range of Delivery Systems: email, voice mail, phone calls, messages, schedules, online forms, dashboards, hard copy reports, handouts, conference rooms, meeting space, and so much more.

Delivery Systems are important, creating value people appreciate and pay for. But like primary products, others can easily copy most improvements in delivery systems. You build a new website shopping cart and your competition quickly follows. If you extend your weekend hours, others will do it too. You open up another branch and guess who opens right next door? You buy an extra truck, and before you know it, they have bought two. Adding value in this category is a perpetual opportunity and a challenge, because customer expectations are rising fast. The Six Levels of Service are always sliding down.

Why is the distinction between Primary Product and Delivery System so essential? It's because people receive one type of value from your Primary Products and a different kind from your Delivery Systems. If you want to keep stepping up as a service provider, you need to work on both.

Your Service Mindset

The first two categories in The BIG Picture focus on your products and your systems. The remaining two categories rely more on the spirit and the actions of your people. How important are these "softer" categories in the *experience* people value? Have you ever walked out of a store that has what you want because the person serving you was rude? Have you ever made a purchase because you really liked the salesperson, not because you needed what he or she was selling?

Service Mindset is the way you meet, greet, and treat other people. This is the realm of professional attitude and spirit, friendliness in the face of frustration, genuine enthusiasm, commitment and care, and compassion for other people. This is a person who gives you his or her undivided attention and tells you to take your time. It's the doctor with a healing bedside manner, the professional from technical support who makes you feel successful, and the colleague who is consistently helpful, optimistic, and upbeat.

The Six Levels of Service apply here too. Someone with a criminal Service Mindset is rude, insulting, and offensive. Staff members laughing at customers with problems. Employees complaining loudly about their jobs. Colleagues making promises they do not keep. A basic Service Mindset is not much better. Service providers who only care about getting paid and leaving early. Untrained employees who show no interest in new learning. Colleagues hoarding information they should share. Expected Service Mindset is routine and nothing special. Service providers who say hello. Employees who say thank you. Colleagues willing to help when you have a question.

As we climb to higher levels, the value of Service Mindset grows. Service providers remember your name and sincerely thank you for your business. Employees are delighted to answer all your questions. Colleagues go out of their way to help each other. Leaders truly walk the talk and demonstrate service passion.

Which of the Six Levels of Service have you recently encountered? Which do you deliver?

Your Ongoing Relationship

An Ongoing Relationship includes your efforts to build connection with customers and colleagues over time. This means staying in touch and thinking longer term, being proactive with recommendations, and following up for feedback. An Ongoing Relationship means recognizing returning customers, rewarding frequent buyers, and expressing your appreciation with loyalty programs, better discounts, and other incentives.

Your commitment to an Ongoing Relationship enriches the present and enhances the future. It is a reliable promise to serve today, and an offer to continue serving tomorrow. Customers get more personalized service, more relevant suggestions, and better product selection. Colleagues get more helpful assistance to succeed in their jobs, receive more appropriate education to grow their careers, and become more satisfied with the work they do each day.

At the criminal level of Ongoing Relationship, a service provider pretends to be concerned about your future, but only cares about his or her own profit. One colleague lies to another. A company sells your personal information without permission. At the basic level, service providers make no effort to remember you or appreciate your business. A colleague takes all the credit instead of sharing it with the team. At the expected level, companies keep track of who you are and what you've purchased. Colleagues help each other using all normal means and methods. At the desired level, you enjoy a membership program, or a coupon for your next purchase. Service providers ask if you are pleased with what you purchased. Colleagues make an extra effort to help each other when really needed—at the end of the month, in a new product launch, or on an important service recovery. At the highest levels of Ongoing Relationship are people deeply committed to your satisfaction and to your success. Colleagues are as interested in your achievements as in their own. Companies will refer you elsewhere if a competitor's offer will serve you better.

The value you enjoy in the category of Ongoing Relationship should not be taken for granted. Many people will serve and sell to you throughout your life. Some will cultivate an ongoing connection and earn your repeat business. These are service providers you want to keep, and the kind you want to be.

Up the Loyalty Ladder

Why is Amazon successful? Because it is creating more value for you in every category of The BIG Picture. Its product range is constantly increasing, its online store is always improving, and its understanding of you and your interests is steadily growing. And, while Amazon cannot provide the same face-to-face attention as Singapore Airlines, Nordstrom, or The Ritz-Carlton Hotel, it demonstrates an attitude of welcome and appreciation for its customers.

This persistent commitment to giving you greater value delivers solid business results: growing volumes, increasing share of market, and record-setting service, satisfaction, and customer loyalty scores.

Loyalty is a special prize in any relationship. It's a hot topic when it comes to customers, but it is equally important when attracting, managing, and retaining great employees. And loyalty delivers substantial benefits with allies and business partners, too: investors, vendors, suppliers, distributors, and resellers.

Different people value different things, but everyone values the same four categories in The BIG Picture. To move anyone up the Loyalty Ladder, the same rules of loyalty apply. Everyone wants fair value for his or her investment of time and money. People want to get what they have requested or think they deserve. Everyone wants to feel welcomed. Everyone wants to be recognized, appreciated, and rewarded.

AMBASSADOR

SUPPORTER

NEUTRAL

DEFECTOR

ADVERSARY

Moving everyone up the Loyalty Ladder makes sense, because anyone can influence people's perception of you and your organization. Anyone can trumpet from the heights of advocacy, or become a horrible adversary overnight. Let's take a closer look.

Adversary: As far as loyalty goes, adversaries are loyal to finding your demise. They are former or current employees who are toxic forces to your other employees. They spread negative rumors about your working conditions, about other people inside your organization, or even about your services and products. Your adversaries may also be customers who feel they have been genuinely wronged. They loudly and publicly complain, post negative information about you online, and actively seek to harm your reputation and your business. Adversarial employees and customers will be highly supportive of your competition, simply because they are your competition. Is recovery of this group worth your energy, time, and investment? What are the costs of doing nothing?

Defector: Defectors have granted their loyalty to someone else. They may be customers who once were complimentary of your service but have since moved on, or they might be employees who left and discovered greater value elsewhere. Defectors won't necessarily say negative things about you, but they promote your competition to anyone who asks. This is the group where a good recovery can transform your former fans into your current evangelists. Refer to chapter 16 on Service Recovery and Guarantees. Your defectors are worth wooing and winning back. Put in the effort and *bounce!*

Neutral: Neutrals aren't loyal to anyone. They may be employees who once loved working for you, and still may work for you, but will leave if they receive a better offer. Because this group is neutral, you can often entice them up the Loyalty Ladder with just a bit of extra value. The key is discovering which bit to offer so you do not waste your resources. And that means paying closer attention to this group, getting to know them better, understanding what they would appreciate in each category of The BIG Picture.

Supporter: Supporters like doing business with you on the inside and the outside. They will promote your business if anyone asks. Employees will say it's a great place to work. Customers will refer you to their family, friends, and business acquaintances—if asked. This group is just one step away from actively promoting you to others, and could easily be converted to genuine ambassador status. But getting them to take that step up means you must step up, too.

Ambassador: Ambassadors are your evangelists, your loyal advocates, and trumpeters. They are the employees who tell others how much they love their job and invite the best of those they meet to join your organization. They are the customers that love you and what you stand for. They give you feedback when you are wrong and defend you when you are right. They will promote you to complete strangers and they will celebrate with you like good friends. Ambassadors will go many extra miles to help you grow and thrive. How far will you go to appreciate and value them?

On every level of the Loyalty Ladder, the next step up comes from creating greater value in at least one of the four categories of The BIG Picture. The next step up always requires action. In an uplifting service culture, responsibility for taking that action belongs to every service leader and every service provider.

Questions for Service Providers

- What is the next step to improve your product knowledge?
- How can you demonstrate an even better Service Mindset?
- How can you deliver more conveniently or quickly?
- What can you do to build a better Ongoing Relationship with your customers and colleagues?

Questions for Service Leaders

- In each category of The BIG Picture, where are you now on the Six Levels of Service? What do your team members say? What do your customers say?
- What percentage of your customers and team members are on each step of the Loyalty Ladder? Which groups do you want to move up the ladder the most? What new action steps will create that uplifting value?

CHAPTER 23

Building Service
Partnerships

What is the difference between completing a project, having a job, and developing your career inside one successful organization? What is the difference between changing money from one currency to another, getting a 30-year mortgage for your home, and consolidating your investment, savings, and credit accounts at a single financial institution? What is the difference between going on a date, going out with the same person for several years, and creating a family together for a lifetime?

These three examples have more in common than you might imagine. In each, the first situation is a transaction with a beginning, a middle, and an ending: completing a project, changing money, and going on a date. You may, or may not, go back again.

The second set of situations are longer term. These relationships are consistent over time: a job, a mortgage, a steady boyfriend or girlfriend. Transactions and relationships are different. Buying a car is a transaction. Bringing the car in for regularly scheduled tune-ups to the same location is a relationship. Installing equipment is a service transaction. A contract for maintenance or regular supplies is a repeating relationship.

The third set of situations are powerful service partnerships, and they grow more important and beneficial over time. In a Powerful Partnership, both parties create and receive greater value. Consolidating your financial life in one place is more convenient for you. Having a larger share of your wallet is more valuable for a financial institution. Developing your career with one great company can be a highway to tremendous achievement. Keeping great employees is essential for every tremendous organization. And what about creating a family, or living together for life? That's partnership on a very personal level, and both parties must invest themselves to keep the partnership growing.

First You Sow, Then You Reap

The key to every successful partnership is both sides giving and receiving greater value. This is true with customers, colleagues, couples, and careers. But there is a catch. The value you want must come from someone else, and the value they want must come from you. So, who goes first?

Service Transaction   Repeating Relationship   Powerful Partnership

Some companies say, "If you become a better customer, then we'll give you better service." Other companies give you better service first, and you reward them with a greater volume of your business.

Some colleagues say, "You scratch my back, and I'll scratch yours." But colleagues who help you succeed without first "making a deal" are ones you will be glad to help the next time they need you. Some employees say, "Give me a raise, and then I will take more responsibility." But big promotions at work rarely happen that way. The person who steps up and takes responsibility earns the raise and recognition.

In a successful partnership, each party is counting on the other to succeed. Each side *wants* the other side to win. Your achievement contributes to the other party's success. A powerful service partnership is win–win at its finest.

How do you continue giving more of whatever someone else appreciates or values? This can be difficult because expectations rise and people's interests change. What worked in the past may not be needed or even wanted in the future.

The Cycle of Service Improvement

The Cycle of Service Improvement is a proven method to discover and deliver higher levels of service. This is the powerful technique behind every well-known service brand. The Cycle of Service Improvement works in all industries, cultures, and countries around the world. It works to improve businesses, governments, and communities. It works when applied to internal and external service situations. The Cycle of Service Improvement works in personal relationships, too. You can use this essential tool to build stronger partnerships in every area of your life.

The Cycle of Service Improvement is a series of four connected conversations. Each requires a different kind of dialogue and another level of commitment. Each stage offers unique opportunities for you to deepen your partnership with other people. You can differentiate from the competition in any of these four quadrants, or you can perform well in all four to distinguish yourself as an extraordinary service provider. Let's examine each stage of this cycle by studying Amazon more closely.

Explore for More

Visit Amazon.com and type in any topic of your choice in the search box. Amazon immediately opens a window into that world for your exploration by listing books, movies, music, and other products related to the topic.

Choose any book and Amazon takes you exploring again. Have a look inside the book. How many people rate the book? How much does it cost? How long will it take for you to get a copy? Scroll down and the exploring continues further. People who bought this book often bought other books at the same time, or changed their mind and bought a different book. Want to know more about those choices? Just click. Still interested in the original book? Then keep scrolling to explore even more useful information. Who wrote it? Who published it? How big is it? What do other readers have to say about it? You can even explore the background of those who wrote the comments.

All this exploration offers tremendous value for you as a customer. And the time you spend exploring gives Amazon value, too. Your time spent on each screen, and your clicks on any image, help the company discover what people like you are interested in, attracted to, and willing to spend your precious time exploring. If you are a repeat visitor, or a customer with an account, then the value to Amazon is even greater. Now it learns exactly what you are interested in at this moment, and it can compare that with whatever you have explored on its website in the past.

This precious information helps Amazon provide even greater value in your next moment of exploration. Suppose you bought a book about hiking from Amazon, and now you are looking for books and movies about traveling in Italy. Before you know it, books about hiking in the Italian Alps will be among the choices on your screen.

Explore means asking open-minded questions and listening carefully to the answers. This is where you build awareness and appreciation for another person's concerns. This is the domain of discovery where new possibilities are invented and revealed.

One example is a financial advisor who listens carefully and works with a terrific list of questions to better understand your dreams, fears, preferences, past experiences, and your current situation. This same advisor does an equally terrific job of helping you understand what he or she does, whom he or she serves, and what he or she stands for and recommends. Another example is a supplier who wants to understand your business better and learn how he or she can help you bring more value to your customers. This same supplier shares with you an outside perspective, industry information, and best-practice case studies you might have never seen. A personal example is the true friend who wants to know what's been going on in your life—where you have been and where you are going—and shares the same about himself or herself with you.

Explore means learning what other people want and need, what they hope for, and would be delighted to experience. What are their goals? What would be a great success? What would be an incredible achievement?

Explore also means uncovering what other people are concerned about, afraid of, and seek to prevent, protect, or avoid. The more you understand what makes people anxious, the better you can serve them. These are the downside possibilities in life. An uplifting service partner explores these, too.

In a powerful partnership, you also want other people to understand you. This means sharing about your history, capabilities, team, resources, and yourself. What do you want to accomplish? How can the customers, colleagues, and companies in your life make a valued contribution to your future?

Unfortunately, many people explore rather poorly. They only listen when someone else bangs the table or argues for attention. They raise their voices in an effort to be heard, instead of listening to understand and waiting patiently for the right moments to speak. They only want to hear the minimum they need for the next step in their process. These people are the order takers in life who care more about how much you buy, and less about what you seek to achieve.

How well do you explore? Are you not really listening, not truly caring, and quickly forgetting what other people tell you? Are you asking the same old questions and following the industry standard? Or are you creating value in the way you engage, and in the quality of discovery you create with other people? Exploration at higher levels requires greater curiosity in both directions, and more concern for the success of others.

How Well Do You Know Your Customers?

Many people think they know who their customers are, but only have a shallow understanding at best. Do you understand your customers' business, what they do, and how they work? Do you know how they measure their success? Do you know the trends, changes, and major issues of their industry? Do you understand your customers' customer, and appreciate how their expectations are changing? Do you know your customers' history, their challenges and achievements, and their next big goal? Do you understand their competition and which companies have a better reputation, larger share, or higher profit margins? Do you know who's who inside their company, who are the people in positions of power, and how to help the people you know succeed? Do you know what your customers think about your organization, your people, and you? Finally, do you understand your customers well enough to stand apart from and above your competition? If that is your goal, then start with better exploration now, before the competition beats you to it.

Coming to Agreement

Explore is the beginning, but understanding each other is not enough. You must confirm the next actions to be taken. The

Agree quadrant is where partners make clear promises to each other about the terms of their relationship: exactly what they will give to and do for each other. Agree does not mean "say yes" to whatever someone else asks for or desires. Agree means "create yes" by working together and reaching an agreement that works for both sides.

Suppose you have chosen the book title you want at Amazon. Do you want the hard copy, paperback, or digital Kindle version? If you chose hard copy, where do you want the book delivered? If you ordered more than one item, do you want them delivered together, or shipped as soon as each one is available? How  would you like to pay for your purchase? With PayPal? With a gift certificate, a coupon, or an existing credit? With a credit card already on file, with a new card you want to enter now, or with an Amazon card you can apply for on the spot?

When you move to checkout, Amazon keeps the value coming by clearly confirming all your choices: the items, prices, delivery addresses, payment method, choice and cost of shipping, gift wrap selection, and your message. Suddenly thought of another item or a different message you want included on the card? Simply go back within a short time after your purchase and you can easily change anything about your order.

Unfortunately, many companies and individuals handle this Agree stage rather badly, viewing it as the mere technicalities of a service agreement. They are rigid and inflexible, earning them a reputation of being bureaucratic and unwilling to provide alternatives. Or they promise the moon but don't document clearly what they promise, and then deliver well below expectations. This is unfortunate, because confusion in this Agree stage of the Cycle leads to disappointment in the stage that follows. Whenever you hear, "But I thought you said . . . ," this means someone did a poor job of coming to a clear agreement.

Other service providers earn a positive service reputation in this quadrant for being easy to do business with, offering alternatives, convenience, and speed. They confirm your commitments with written notice and thorough and accurate documentation.

The Agree quadrant is rich with opportunities for you to step up your service. Can you offer greater flexibility or a wider range of choices? Can you simplify your contracts, or explain your terms in a more engaging manner? Can you make your promises accurate, comprehensive, or clear?

A Playful Policy Review

Most frontline staff members are taught to follow policies and procedures. They may be hesitant to break the rules to improve their service, yet some rules should be broken, changed, or at least seriously bent from time to time. If your customers complain about rigid policies and robotic staff, you can make a change and make a difference with a playful policy review.

Bring your team together and set the mood for fun. Send a cartoon invitation, put a funny sign in the room, wear party hats, or enjoy a short video of a comedian's great performance. Then, keeping the mood light and easy, share a list of your current policies and procedures while asking these three key questions:

- What do you like least about this policy or procedure?
- What do our customers find most difficult or problematic?
- How would you change this policy if you could?

After the meeting, change what you can to improve the experience for your customers and your team. If a policy cannot be changed (and there may be good reasons not to), then make an extra effort to explain the reasons more clearly.

The Special Case of "What If?"

The Explore and Agree stages offer a unique opportunity to step up your service by anticipating what could go wrong and putting contingency plans in place. But many service providers, especially those in sales, routinely ignore this opportunity. The last thing many salespeople want to do is discuss potential problems when they are about to close a deal. But by raising the awkward question, "What if?" a service provider can actually uplift a client's confidence and increase their ultimate satisfaction.

You may have heard the expression "firefighting" used at work. This means something unexpected has happened, and now people are running around with great haste and waste, putting out the fires. Whether you are a customer or a service provider, putting out fires is rarely a happy situation. By asking, "What if?" and by exploring and agreeing in advance, you can prevent these fires even before they start.

Imagine you are in charge of organizing an annual company event where you will honor your finest service providers and many of your most important customers will be attending. You meet with two five-star hotels to discuss your needs. Both offer a similar menu, a poolside gathering before the dinner, comparable decorations, and an almost identical price. The first hotel's representative gives you a tour, answers your questions, and hands you a proposal. The representative says, "We're sure your program is going to be a great success, and we hope you will choose us for this event." The representative at the second hotel says and does the exact same thing. But as you are about to leave she asks, "May I talk to you about one more thing before you go?" You are surprised by this last-minute question and wonder what is on her mind. She continues, saying, "The poolside gathering before dinner is a great idea, and I am sure your guests will love it. Rain is rather unlikely at this time of year, but just in case, may I take a moment to tell you about our plans?" Now you nod with interest.

"We always watch the weather carefully before an important event like yours," she says. "If it does rain, we will move your poolside gathering inside to the ballroom lobby. Rain also means your guests will be a bit delayed, so we'll move the schedule back an extra fifteen minutes. We'll take care of this with the kitchen and the banquet servers so you don't need to be concerned about it. And we will provide valet parking for your guests as a small way of making them feel good, even if the weather is not so good." She smiles and concludes with, "I don't think it's going to rain, but I did think you would feel more comfortable knowing about our plans, just in case. Are these plans OK with you?"

Is there any question which hotel you will choose? The other hotel may have exactly the same plans in case of rain, but if its representative doesn't take the time to tell you about it, he or she didn't create the extra value. And here's an unexpected bonus: even if it does not rain, your confidence in the service provider who asked will still go up. Why? Because they explored the downside possibilities and then agreed with you on an uplifting service solution.

Do you explore what might go wrong with your customers and colleagues? Do you take the time to discuss alternatives, make contingency and backup plans just in case they are needed? Or are you hoping that everything will work out fine and you will not have to put out any fires?

Delivering Uplifting Service

The Deliver stage is where you keep the promises you make and fulfill conditions as agreed. Or you can go the extra mile, providing a surprising level of service. Promised a speedy one-week delivery to someone in a hurry? Call after three days to let the client know his or her delivery is ready. Guaranteed a certain level of power or performance? Make your guarantee, plus 10 percent, the minimum you deliver. Offered to provide hands-on support? Be there to hold the client's hand much more frequently than he or she expected.

In this quadrant there is an unexpected opportunity lurking in the phenomenon of people chasing other people. Do you ever chase your colleagues or service providers for updates or information? Do other people ever have to chase you for a detail or report? Chasing each other with calls and messages is very common, but it's not very welcome to either party. To the person being chased, it can be a hassle or a nuisance. To the person who is chasing, the information he or she is seeking is already later than expected, which is why it is called "chasing." You can deliver uplifting service by informing others in advance instead of others chasing you.

Ship a package with any of the big courier companies, and the first thing they will do is scan the barcode. From that moment until the moment your package is delivered, you can easily track progress on its website, or receive updates on your phone or by email. You can always know where your package is, where it was, when it left, and where it's going. Many customers value this information for the peace of mind it provides, even though it does not affect the delivery time or date.

When things go wrong, providing proactive information is of even greater service value. When Singapore Airlines flights are delayed at the last minute by air traffic control or because of technical issues, passengers may already be at the gate or onboard the plane. Throughout these unexpected situations, the airline keeps its passengers well informed. At regular intervals a representative provides the latest update and makes a promise when the next update will be provided. Even if nothing has changed by that time and no new information is available, an airline representative communicates on schedule. This reliable communication means that passengers are never left wondering or uninformed. In fact, this simple tactic during flight delays has become a steady source of compliments.

Proactive communication is appreciated, even if it does not improve or change a situation. But proactive communication does not mean calling someone over and over again or sending him or her messages nonstop. That could be annoying. Some people will appreciate a daily report; others, a weekly summary.

Some want notice as each milestone is met; others, only if a milestone is missed. Some prefer updates by email; others, by phone or by text. Some want to hear from you personally; others want you to contact their assistants, unless the situation is unexpected or unique.

With so many variables, how can you figure out the right amount of proactive information to deliver at what time and through what medium of communication? Apply the lessons in this chapter. First, explore the situations that may arise, the schedules, the people, and options for being in touch. Second, agree when communication should be proactive, which details will be included, and what timing and technologies you will employ. Third, deliver the information that you promised. Get in touch before someone else comes chasing you. Be an uplifting service provider by keeping your customers and colleagues up-to-date.

Assure Closes the Loop

The fourth stage in the Cycle of Service Improvement is Assure— follow up and check for satisfaction, making sure what you agreed to and delivered was fully appreciated and effective.

Everything can be improved, even your proactive communication. What was appropriate at one moment may no longer be what another person appreciates or desires. For example, your customer may have asked for an update every Tuesday and she valued your weekly communication. But after a

while, your weekly message has become a nuisance. She would prefer a monthly summary, with a weekly report to her assistant. But how will you know unless she tells you? And when will she tell you unless you ask? You will learn about this change in expectations, and a great deal more, when you step up and assure. Imagine what you might learn by asking. "Do the actions that we take still address your concerns? Does the service we provide give you the value that you need? Is the agreement we made before still the best for your current situation?"

Some people handle the Assure quadrant badly. They say, "If you have a problem, give me a call." And then they hope you do not call, thinking, "No news is good news." But no news is bad news in the service business, because a happy customer who never tells you about it can be stolen away by someone else and an unhappy customer often will not tell you, but will tell many other people.

Asking the Ultimate Question

The ultimate question in the Assure quadrant closes the loop and starts another successful cycle. This powerful sentence connects the end of one service experience to the beginning of another: "Is there anything we could do differently the next time that would make our service better or more valuable for you?"

This question tells customers you are looking to the future, seeking to improve, and are grateful for their feedback. It shows that you are committed to taking measures to improve or increase their satisfaction. This is refreshing for customers and can be vital for your business. A question like this will open the dialogue for greater productivity between departments, better collaboration on teams, and even a closer connection with family members.

The next time you complete a job, finish a project, or think your delivery is complete, don't wait for the next opportunity. Initiate the conversation to serve better and make your business stronger. Some say it's the other person's job to tell you if his or her needs have changed. But that's the difference between a transaction, a relationship, and a partnership that is growing. In a Powerful Partnership, you aren't satisfied that your partner is content. You want to know what more you can do together and how you can improve.

Every Completed Cycle Builds Trust

Each time you complete a cycle of Explore, Agree, Deliver, and Assure, more trust develops between you and other people in your business, your community, and your personal life. Discover what others care about, are concerned about, or want to make happen in their lives. Explore. Make promises to take action on their behalf. Be responsible for some aspect of their well-being. Agree. Then do what you promised to do and keep in contact during the process. Deliver. Finally, follow up and follow through to make sure they are fully satisfied with your actions. Assure.

Building trust often starts with small promises, less exposure, and lower risk. A customer orders just a few before she orders more, and buys a few more times before she considers you her sole supplier. An employer gives out smaller projects first, discovering who delivers, then increases the importance of projects and budgets over time.

This makes sense in business, but also applies in your personal, social, and community life. Building trust with others is the outcome of uplifting service. It is the glue we need for our partnerships today, and those we create for the future.

Keep the Fire Burning

It was late. Todd Nordstrom was sitting in the boardroom of my office looking out the window. He was eating an apple. I could tell he was winding down for his early flight out of Singapore and back to America the next morning.

"What happens when it's not new anymore?" he asked.

"What do you mean?" I responded.

He took another bite and held up his pointer finger as if to signal he needed a second to swallow.

"How do companies like Marina Bay Sands, NTUC Income, and Changi Airport maintain the enthusiasm after the education?" he asked. "It's got to diminish, right?"

I pushed my chair back from the table. "The enthusiasm can be lost over time," I said. "But, that typically doesn't happen if people truly grasp the reasons for uplifting service."

"What do you mean by that?" Todd asked.

I chuckled and reminded him of his visits. "Did you see how happy it makes those people to provide uplifting service?"

Todd took another bite of his apple as he smiled. Then he spun around in his chair—almost childlike. His smile grew as he crunched on his bite of apple.

"When was the last time you did something special for your wife or one of your kids?" I asked. "You know, one of those times when

253

they are surprised and you were just as excited to see the expression on their face?"

"I am hoping the gifts I bring back from this trip will make them smile," he said. "I bought my daughter a sarong kebaya so she can dress up like a member of the Singapore Airlines crew. And I got my son a sepak takraw ball. He'll be surprised to see a rattan version of the beanbag he and his buddies kick around.

"I wasn't quite sure what to get my wife . . ." His voice drifted off, and he was clearly thinking about his family at home. "I've been sending back pictures, and I bought her one of those nice gold-dipped orchids, but those seem like such small things compared to the whole experience of visiting this place."

"The reward for you is in the service," I said. "But you've got to keeping taking the next step up. You've got to keep that fire of service burning brightly."

He nodded.

"Why don't you bring your wife with you to Singapore on your next visit, Todd?" I asked.

His eyes opened widely as the idea took him by surprise, and then he nodded as it became realistic. "We have been exploring a trip together, and we are thinking about visiting Asia. We just hadn't really agreed yet on when or where to go." Then he leaned back in his chair and smiled. He was thinking about the future with his wife, already creating the next conversation.

Questions for Service Providers

- You will get what you want by helping other people get what they want. What can you do to provide better service for your customers? What can you do to be a better partner for your colleagues? How can you create more value for your organization?

Questions for Service Leaders

- Apply the Six Levels of Service to the Cycle of Service Improvement. How well does your organization currently Explore, Agree, Deliver, and Assure?
- How can you build more powerful and valuable partnerships with your customers, suppliers, employees, and community?

CHAPTER 24

Taking Personal Responsibility

Imagine you are at work and something unexpected goes wrong. Your customer is frustrated and your colleagues are upset. The boss is disturbed and you are feeling anxious. You are already late on another project and the policy in this case is unclear. This is an uncomfortable situation.

Can you sense the pressure, feel the stress, and hear the voices rising? Now, fill in the blanks with whatever first comes to mind.

    It's not my _____.
    I don't have _____.
    Our policy isn't _____.
    I'm sorry, but _____.

If you are like many people, you may have found yourself mentally filling in words like these:

    It's not my *fault.*
    I don't have *time to fix this.*

Our policy isn't *clear*.

I'm sorry, but *I can't do anything right now.*

When things go wrong, it's always possible to point a finger, make excuses, or feel badly about the problem. These reactions are common. And, they are highlighted in the media every day through accusations, allegations, guilty verdicts, and stories of shame, blame, and victimization.

But in the world of uplifting service, blaming other people doesn't help. Feeling badly about what went wrong doesn't make it any better. Finding excuses and justifications doesn't improve a thing.

Uplifting Service Champions

Uplifting Service Champions choose a different approach, taking responsibility for difficult situations—and taking action to improve them. They solve problems that arise every day, and then look for more problems to solve. When a customer is dissatisfied, they say, "I will fix this for you." If a project is running late, they take ownership to make it

right. Instead of blaming or shaming inactive colleagues, they empower and inspire them to action. Service Champions don't blame circumstances; they look for steps forward. They are unwilling to be stranded in the viewpoint of a victim. They create empowering perspectives and positive experiences each day.

Service Champions fill in the blanks with deliberately different answers:

It's not my *style to blame other people.*
I don't have *time to argue about the past. I am creating the future.*
Our policy isn't *going to stop me from making this right.*
I'm sorry, *but we will solve this problem for you.*

Uplifting Service Champions build teamwork, increase pride, improve communication, and make our world a better place by serving others. They are people, just like you, who take responsibility and make real improvements. When you see something that should be done, you do it. When you notice something that could be better, you recommend it. When you see an opportunity to step up and serve, you don't hesitate—you take it.

The Five Styles of Service

Service Champions take personal responsibility for other people's *experience* of the service they provide. This point of view recognizes that service is not only what you say or do, it is what someone else values from your actions. Service champions modify their style to suit the other person and the situation, using the Five Styles of Service to make this happen. These Five Styles of Service are not higher or lower levels, or better or worse; they are simply different. And, during the course of a Service Transaction with many Perception Points, each of these five styles may be the appropriate to use at different moments in time.

Direction: Direction is telling other people exactly what to do, giving them clear instructions and expecting them to follow. A police officer directing traffic is delivering a service. A physical therapist gives instructions so patients are not injured in a work-out. An IT consultant says to you on the phone, "I want you to type in the following commands, and then tell me what you see on the screen." That style is direction and, in the right situation, it is excellent service.

Production: This style of service focuses on getting the job done efficiently and quickly. It's common between colleagues who are both familiar with the work. It's also the right style to use when someone is in a hurry. Scan the barcode, pack the item, close the ticket, and say good-bye. This is the pizza chain promising delivery within 45 minutes. It's the tailor or dry cleaner offering same day service. It's the grocer offering a freshness guarantee. This style of service can be attractive for service providers because it gets a lot done quickly. But to some customers this can appear robotic and bureaucratic—more focused on your procedures than on the experience you are creating.

Education: This style of service teaches and informs. It helps people learn more about what is happening and appreciate why you are serving them the way you do. "Let me show you how that works. Allow me to explain. Here's what you can do to get the best results." The education style of service makes other people information-rich. It empowers them to become better customers for you. You may not be a teacher, but consider how many opportunities you have to serve others well by helping them understand a range of products, prepare for steps in a process, or get more value from the choices they have made. Doctors who teach their patients see higher compliance rates because people take their medication as prescribed, and enjoy lower malpractice rates because patients sue these doctors far less often. Governments that explain their policies enjoy higher levels of citizen support. And in any arena where products are commoditized and prices are easily matched, the service provider who teaches and informs can earn a competitive edge.

Motivation: This style of service is an acknowledging pat on the back. A personal trainer who pushes you to keep going in the gym then praises your sweaty effort. The technician who says, "Don't worry, you called the right place. I can help you." This simple phrase lifts your spirits up as he calms you down. Or you complimenting your own customer with a few simple and encouraging words: "You made a good choice."

Motivation is also the style to use to make an upset customer feel right, even when they are wrong. Sometimes customers mix up the facts, don't understand the policy, or have exaggerated beyond belief. But the last thing upset customers want to hear is anyone saying, "You're wrong." What they want to hear is that you understand, appreciate, and agree with them on what they value. And you can do this with a motivating style of service.

An upset customer says, "Your employees are rude and unprofessional." And you reply, "You are right to expect courteous and professional staff." No argument. Your customer says, "Your policies are rigid. Your company is bureaucratic." And you reply, "I agree that we should be as flexible and user-friendly as possible. Your suggestions can help." Suddenly you are on the same side. Your customer says, "This product isn't what I was promised. And your price is way too high!" You reply, "You have a right to be satisfied by whatever you purchase from us. And you deserve good value for your money. Let's review what you have purchased and see if there's a better option."

These responses make your customer *feel* right without making you wrong. By actively agreeing on the importance of what someone else values, you give them an emotional pat on the back. This makes him or her feel better, and makes it easier for you to work together, too. The next time you want to avoid an argument, try this approach with your partner or your spouse.

Inspiration: Inspiration is a style of service that makes a genuine person-to-person connection. It lets people know you are interested in their well-being, not just in their wallet. This style sets the tone for caring about others, welcoming others into your world, and appreciating the opportunity to enter theirs. This style is starting with "Good morning! Nice to see you" and ending with "Thank you for this opportunity to serve you." This is the heartfelt human spirit that uplifts other people, and in the process uplifts you.

The style you use will depend on the situation. Who are you serving, what do they want, and what style will they value? People in a hurry want production. The curious customer appreciates education. Someone who is confused may value clear direction. Those who are just learning will enjoy a shot of motivation. And everyone from time to time simply wants to be seen and heard as a unique or special person, a service you can provide with a moment of inspiration.

The Other Side of Customer Service

Much of the domain of customer service focuses on being a better service provider. But there is another side of customer service, and that is being a better customer. An Uplifting Service Champion takes personal responsibility for this side as well. When you give great service, customers appreciate you more. When you give bad service, customers can be a pain in the neck. Similarly, when you are an appreciative and considerate customer, service providers will often go the extra mile to serve you better. But if you rant and pound the table, people may serve you grudgingly, if at all. Here are proven steps you can take to be a better customer and enjoy *receiving* better service:

1. **Be appreciative and polite.** Remember, there is a fellow human being on the other end of your phone call, the receiving side of your email, or just across the counter. Begin each interaction with a quick "Hi. Thank you for helping me. I really appreciate it." This takes about two seconds and can dramatically improve the mood of a service provider.

2. **Get your service provider's name and use it.** You can make this short and friendly by first offering your name and then asking, "Who am I speaking with please?" or if you are face-to-face, simply, "May I know your name?" Once you know it, repeat it with a smile in your voice. This creates a personal connection and makes it much harder for a service provider to treat you like an anonymous account holder or policy number.

3. **Be upbeat.** Many service providers face customer after customer all day long. The routine can become tiresome. When an energetic and smiling customer appears, that person often enjoys special care and treatment in return. What you send out does come back. Attitudes—positive and negative—really are contagious.

4. **Provide information just the way they want it.** Many service providers need your data in a sequence that fits their forms, screens, and procedures. Have all your information ready to go, but give it in the order they prefer. Saying, "I have all my information ready. Which would you like first?" lets the provider know you are prepared and will be easy to work with. The time you take getting everything in order will save time in the service conversation, too.

5. **Confirm next actions**. Repeat what your service provider promises to do. Confirm dates, times, amounts, promises,

responsibilities, and commitments. This helps you move together through the service process, catching any misunderstanding and correcting it along the way. Be sure you both understand what will happen next: what they will do, what you will do, and what both parties have agreed to going forward.

6. **When appropriate, commiserate.** Sometimes service providers let their frustration show. A slow computer, a previous customer, high call volume, pressure from a manager, or some unwelcome personal event may have upset them. When you hear an upset tone, be the one to soothe it. "It sounds like things are tough right now. I really appreciate your help." This brief moment of empathy can be an oasis in their world.

7. **Show your appreciation.** A sincere "thank you" is always appropriate. If your service provider deserves more, give more. A nicely written compliment can make a huge difference in someone else's day, or career. And who knows? The person you praise today may serve you again tomorrow.

Service is a two-way street. The traffic of goodwill flows equally between customers and service providers. If you want to enjoy uplifting service, don't wait for someone else to make your day. Take the first step by extending your own goodwill.

What's in It for You?

Stepping up to improve your service can mean a lot of work. Upgrading your actions and uplifting your attitude is a real commitment. Should you bother? Before completing this section of the book, let's be candid and ask the question: "What's in it for you?"

If you do step up, customers will appreciate your uplifting service. And you'll enjoy more compliments. Happy customers come back and they tell other people. That's good for your organization and builds job security. That is good for you. If you upgrade your service to colleagues, your efforts may well be noticed. What goes around does come around. When you step up for colleagues, they are more likely to step up for you. That makes your work easier and the place you work more satisfying for everyone. And what about everyone else in your business network: suppliers, distributors, and other organizations? Serve them better and they will serve you better, too.

This two-way street even applies to those in your personal life: your family, friends, neighbors, and everyone else you meet. We all live and work in a whole world of relationships based on service. As you uplift and upgrade the service you provide, the world will uplift you.

Questions for Service Providers

- Where can you take more personal responsibility at work, at home, and in your life?
- Which styles of service are you most comfortable providing?
- How can you choose the best style to use with different customers and in different service situations?

Questions for Service Leaders

- Where do you hear the sound of blame, shame, and excuses in your organization?
- How can you be a role model of taking personal responsibility?
- Which styles of service do your employees provide most often? Which styles do your customers prefer?
- Which styles do you use most frequently when engaging with your team members? Which styles do they appreciate most? Which are most effective?

SECTION FIVE

DRIVE

CHAPTER 25

Your Implementation Roadmap

We were on a wooded trail leading up the side of a small mountain in Washington State. It was summer. My parents—both in their late 70s at the time—had invited me to join them on a two-hour hike to the top. We were halfway to the summit, appropriately prepared for the challenge and the season with hiking boots, long pants, jackets, and hats. We paused for a moment to admire the quiet beauty, tall pine trees, and the cooling high-altitude breeze.

Suddenly, a young man with intense focus came charging up the trail. He wore nothing but running shoes, gym shorts, and a sweat-soaked T-shirt. We barely had time to step aside as he sprinted past us, literally racing to the summit. I could hardly believe my eyes.

"He's running all the way up this trail?" I asked in disbelief. My parents smiled and nodded. They are frequent hikers and had seen this many times before. "Yes, some people actually run the en-tire way, driving themselves to do it in the shortest possible time," my mother explained. "Others stop along the way to take pic-tures or to rest. We like to keep a steady rhythm. But one thing is certain: it doesn't matter what your pace is, this trail takes everyone to the top."

The path you have followed in this book is as reliable as that mountain trail. Follow the steps and keep on going, and you will reach the summit of uplifting service. The architecture is proved, the principles and practices work, and the framework provides a structure for your self-assessment and next actions. But the culture of every organization is unique. And the way you implement what's inside this book will be completely unique for you.

You may want to charge up the hill, implementing many new practices in rapid succession. Or you may plan a longer ascent with many stages to accomplish. Some organizations are climbing the steep slope from a low base of upset customers and a poor service reputation. If this is where you are today, take heart, take action, and this path will bring you up. Others are in the middle of their fields—neither the service champion nor the worst. If this is where you find yourself, you can walk this path with confidence. It will take you to even higher service levels. Some companies and cultures are already strong and well known for uplifting service. If this is where you are today, congratulations. But you know that your competition is climbing higher every day. Stay in shape and stay on top by applying the principles and practices in this book.

Preparing Your Implementation Roadmap

Whenever my parents embark on a new hiking adventure, they find out before they go what other hikers have experienced on their chosen trails. What is recommended? What is to be avoided? What preparations are most important? What will make their hikes ahead successful and satisfying? My parents study key features of the trail. They learn what to bring and what to leave behind. They figure out in advance the best time to start, how far to go, what to do when the weather is nice, and do differently if it turns nasty.

Now you can do the same. Using this Implementation Roadmap, let's look ahead to see what awaits you and how you can best prepare for a successful culture-building journey.

Many people want to know how long it takes to build or improve a service culture. From my experience with organizations of all sizes and from all over the world, the answer is 12 months. This does not mean that everything will be completely different one year from today. It means that even a very large organization with a well-established culture can see a positive shift toward service improvement and service results within one year.

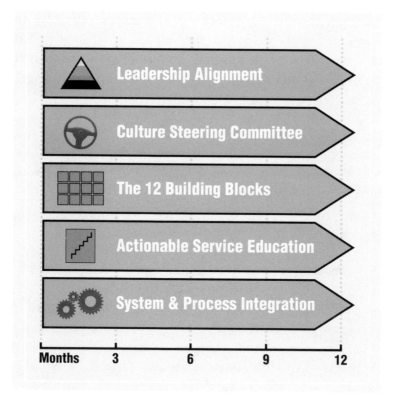

And a smaller, faster, or more nimble organization can make a dramatic change in the same amount of time.

Whether your implementation is fast and focused, or more gradual and steady, you can succeed by looking ahead in five key areas.

1. Leadership Alignment

Building or improving a service culture requires commitment from the top. But buy-in alone is not enough. Your leadership team members must be aligned with each other. They must understand why uplifting service is a key to the future and what will be required of them as leaders—and as a team—on this rewarding and demanding journey.

Leadership alignment provides a healthy start on the path and ensures strong support down the road when you need it. Until this alignment is clear and strong, avoid raising expectations with others. Do not announce a service improvement initiative until your leaders are ready to back these words with action.

How do you know if your leadership team is ready? Pose these questions to your team at the top, and then listen for discussion and debate. Keep the conversation going until the team aligns and comes to a clear agreement.

- Why build an uplifting service culture?
- What are the results we commit to achieve?
- How will we provide leadership support?
- Who will be on the Steering Committee?
- When and where will we begin this project? Who will be involved when we start?
- How will we expand, refine, and sustain this long-term effort?
- How will we measure success and share the recognition and rewards?

2. Service Culture Steering Committee

Building or improving the service culture in an organization is a holistic project that touches everyone. Create a Steering Committee to plan and guide this project. This committee will gather support, schedule activities, review results, and make recommendations or revisions to the roadmap.

Committee members must represent the concerns and interests of everyone in the organization. Representatives from human resources, organization development, sales, service delivery, and customer care will all understand the need for their involvement from the beginning. But other parts of the organization have different points of view and valuable perspectives to share. Include representative voices from the frontline operations, production, logistics, research, finance, legal, facilities, supervisors, managers, leaders, and unions. Your committee may change or rotate members from time to time. Fresh talent is good for the work of this group and for the careers of those involved. Creating your Steering Committee means answering questions such as:

- Who will serve on the Steering Committee, and for how long?
- How often will the Steering Committee meet? What will be on the Committee's agenda?
- What decision-making power will the Committee have, and how much budget will they control?
- Who can the Committee call on for expertise, sponsorship, or support?
- How will the Committee evaluate their effectiveness?
- How will an individual's participation in the Steering Committee be recognized and rewarded?

The answers to these questions will be as diverse as organizations themselves. By exploring, agreeing, delivering, and assuring, you will discover the best answers for your organization to achieve your own objectives.

3. The 12 Building Blocks

The next step in your Implementation Roadmap is a self-assessment in each of The 12 Building Blocks of Service Culture. For each building block, use these questions to guide your exploration:

- Why is this building block useful for us?
- How clear is our focus?
- What are we doing in this area now?
- How well are these activities and programs working?
- Who is responsible here? Who else should be involved?
- What could be improved? How hard would that be?
- How much impact or value would be created?
- What are the next steps up?
- How can this building block be better connected to the others?

You may discover some current activities are out of synch with where you want to go. These legacy policies and practices are reminders of "the way we've always done it." Leaving these remnants in place sends a confusing message. Out-of-date practices should be stopped early in your journey.

You may also find opportunities to spotlight service with very little effort. Sometimes a minor tweak or simple step can send a very supportive signal. For example, celebrating customer compliments can be done immediately and at low cost. Publicizing service improvements requires very little effort and makes everyone feel good. Actions like these are low-hanging fruit. You can pluck them early and enjoy.

In some building blocks, improvements and new activities may require substantial investment. For example, revising your recruitment, appraisal, or promotion strategy takes leadership time and attention. Revamping your customer satisfaction or loyalty metrics is not a simple project. Launching a new contest requires ongoing commitment and possibly financial resources. Improvements in these areas may not be quick or cheap. But your investments of attention, time, and money can deliver powerful and lasting results.

The more you study The 12 Building Blocks of Service Culture, the more opportunities you will see. But don't do everything you see as fast as you possibly can. Rather, stage your activities over time—it's a roadmap, not a race. Send an early message, and then reinforce it another way. Focus attention on a service issue, and then highlight the same issue through a completely different channel. Refine your activities, revise your programs, review what works and do it again. Make the message consistent and compelling, but keep your initiatives fresh, engaging, and even entertaining.

4. Actionable Service Education

With leadership aligned, a Steering Committee in place, and building block activities prepared, you are ready to cascade Actionable Service Education into and across the entire organization. The application of these principles will be different in each job and every function, but the principles themselves are the same. This common application of fundamental service principles is essential for building a strong service culture. This kind of education brings new insights and understanding; it calls for reflection and questioning of current views and practices. This kind of education asks every person to put new learning into action, and it requires full support from all—leaders, managers, supervisors, and frontline staff.

Leading these educational courses and conversations is a tremendous responsibility. This unique role is course leader, educator, facilitator, coach, encourager, problem-solver, consultant, and provocateur all in one. These individuals should be carefully selected for their understanding, attitude, and orientation to new action. This role calls for patience, clarity of thinking, commitment to uplifting service, and boundless generosity in the encouragement of others. It is a unique opportunity to influence the views and lives of others, and to have one's own life enriched in the process.

I frequently encourage CEOs to enable their own team members to lead in-house service education programs. And I encourage team members to volunteer to become these course leaders. External training providers rarely understand your business concerns and objectives as your employees. This is another common reason why so many customer service training programs don't produce substantial or sustainable results. Your goal is more than short-term improvements in a few problem service areas. You want to build an organization with an internal capability to solve problems today and create great successes in the future.

Course leaders influence other people's actions and thus shape the future of the entire organization. Anyone in this position should connect early with the managers of the employees they are teaching. This early connection is essential to ensure a course leader is well prepared. It opens a channel for course leaders to learn about current issues and bring them into each class. It also allows course leaders to return after the class with feedback and practical suggestions for the managers.

Anytime someone participates in a class of actionable service education, he or she should be engaged and informed in advance to understand these questions:

- Why have you been selected?
- What will you be learning?

- How will this learning apply to your job?
- What new actions will be expected from you?
- What value will your new actions help create?
- How will your actions and results be measured?
- What support can you expect from your manager?
- How can you share ideas for further improvement?

Cascading Actionable Service Education throughout an organization requires a rollout of some proportion. Use this mobilization to reinforce other service culture building efforts. For example, bring yesterday's Voice of the Customer comments and last month's Service Measures and Metrics into tomorrow's problem-solving sessions. Harness the ideas and action plans from today's class discussions into next week's Service Improvement Process. Study last month's service award winners to understand how they put service principles into action. Keep fresh information flowing into your service education process. Keep new ideas for action flowing out. Keep the energy for improvement moving and growing in all directions.

5. System and Process Integration

Ultimately, the principles of Actionable Service Education can be embedded into your processes and daily procedures. The objective of System and Process Integration is for these principles to penetrate the very way you work so that simply coming to work and doing your work provides inescapable service education.

For example, at Vopak terminals in Asia, every incoming customer complaint is tracked along a well-developed Service Transaction and Perception Point map. This map guides the quality and sequence of actions to ensure a positive customer experience. At Parkway Health, the hospital operating system includes a standard procedure that charts Service Transactions and Perception Points on the Six Levels of Service in each category of The BIG Picture. At Wipro, in preparation for customer satisfaction reviews, customer teams prepare by using Explore, Agree, Deliver, Assure: the Cycle of Service Improvement. And at Xerox Emirates, the *Bounce!* model and the Loyalty Ladder underpin every opportunity for service recovery and service improvement. With tools like these in use every day, the distinctions and practices of uplifting service are embedded in daily action and deeply into the culture.

Where can you adopt the language in this book so it becomes the language of your team? How can you apply the models in this book to uplift and upgrade the service you provide?

Review each process involving customers and service providers. There are many to consider where you work. For example:

- How are customers greeted?
- How is product and service information presented?
- How are the needs and concerns of customers identified?
- How are service orders clarified and confirmed?
- How is service tracked and delivered?
- How are customers kept informed?
- How is satisfaction checked? How is value measured?
- How do you follow-up and follow-through?
- How do you deepen relationships with customers?
- How is learning captured and shared inside the organization?

In each case, where can you apply the principles of Actionable Service Education? Where can you use the Common Service Language? How can you create connections with the building blocks of service culture? Embedding these into your systems and processes helps everyone progress along the proven path.

Often things go well and sometimes better than expected. Other times, projects run aground despite the best of ideas and intentions. What can you do to increase the odds of success and minimize the likelihood of trouble? You can study those who succeeded before you, and those who did not. You can learn from the experience of others, as you will see in the next chapter.

CHAPTER 26

Learning from Experience

Karen was young and curious and wanted to know what was inside the box. Why did grandfather always make a point of putting it on the top shelf outside her reach? What was she not supposed to handle? She watched and waited until one day he left the small box lying on the table. It was a mistake and Karen knew it, but she said nothing to her grandfather. Instead, she waited patiently for him to leave the room.

She picked up the box and shook it, her little hands trembling with excitement. One side slid open and many small sticks fell out. They were colorful on one end and just the right size for her fingers. Karen rolled them back and forth in her hands, admiring the bright red bits on the ends, sliding them happily in and out of the box.

Then it happened in an instant, a spark, a flash, and a flame erupting in her fingers. It seared her skin with no warning, and she ran away, screeching in pain.

Grandpa came charging around the corner. He was alarmed by her scream. Immediately he smelled and saw the reason. He stomped out the small fire on the carpet that already threatened to spread. Then he swept Karen up in his arms and they cried together. She cried from the pain of learning the hard way. He cried from knowing that keeping the box out of her reach was a proven strategy for safety, and leaving it within her grasp was almost a disaster.

Matches are concentrated energy. They can light a candle or a campfire. They can also ignite an inferno. Building an uplifting service culture also requires energy and great concentration. Success illuminates everyone it touches. Failure can be painful and expensive. How do you reconcile your vision, passion, and aspirations with the politics, realities, and constraints of an organization? What are the proven steps to follow? What are the difficulties and disasters you must avoid?

For more than two decades, I have been working on uplifting service programs with clients all over the world. Many have succeeded, some far beyond expectations. Others have stalled or delivered less than expected. Experience is a wonderful teacher, especially when you can learn from mistakes made by someone else. Learning from experience shortens your own learning curve, so you can do what works sooner, and avoid what doesn't work altogether.

> "Wisdom is the daughter of experience."
>
> *Leonardo da Vinci*

Don't Sell Snow to the Eskimos

Where is the right place to start a service improvement program inside your organization? The answer may seem obvious. You start with team members who sell to and serve your customers. After all, customers are the ones who buy your products and use your services. They come back when they are happy and complain when they are not. It makes sense that salespeople, delivery teams, and support and service representatives should be the first to participate in a service improvement program, right?

Well, no. If your objective is to build an uplifting service culture, this approach is very problematic.

It's true that people in "customer-facing" roles are closest to your customers on a daily basis. They already understand that service is important. They know that upset customers complain. They know happy customers are easier to serve. And they know from experience that only satisfied customers come back, buy again, buy more, and recommend their friends. Customer-facing team members have many incentives to serve your customers well. And they may very well be doing the best they can, under the circumstances.

When you provide new service education, greater encouragement, and more recognition for this team, they will be inspired to serve better, smile wider, and strive even harder to delight. But at some point (and possibly quite quickly), they will bump against the constraints of your current systems, budget, or procedures. At some point they will start to wonder how they can give customers better service if their colleagues do not give them better service. How can they go the extra mile when they don't get support they need from their colleagues around the organization?

And they have a point! Asking customer-facing team members to give better service before they get better service from those behind the scenes is a recipe for disappointment for both parties. This approach not only frustrates those serving customers in front; it also upsets team members in the back who don't understand why their colleagues are always asking for more. So they push back, which frustrates those in front even further. It's an unfortunate and unnecessary lose–lose situation.

Now compare this with an alternative approach. Suppose you begin by focusing service improvement efforts on your internal service providers. Imagine the finance and legal departments offering to make things easier for those who sell and close new deals? Imagine teams in production and manufacturing going out of their way to make things faster or more flexible for those who see the customers each day. Imagine warehouse, logistics, and delivery departments doing everything they can to help their colleagues serve customers even better. Imagine software developers asking software resellers what they could do to make the job easier. Imagine how welcome this offer would be for those who face your customers, clients, and competition every day. Imagine their surprise and delight.

Then what happens when you ask these front-facing team members to serve their customers better than ever? With surprising service coming from the inside, it's easier to step up your service on the outside. When front-facing team members come up with new ideas and turn around to seek support, they find colleagues able and eager to assist. Why? Because those internal service colleagues were educated and inspired to provide better service first.

When launching an uplifting service program, don't start with only customer-facing team members. It would be much better to begin with internal service providers: production and design, hardware and software, warehousing and logistics, facilities, finance, legal, IT, and HR. Or start both groups together—and teach them together—for end-to-end service commitment. Let those on the inside inspire those who are serving on the outside.

It's a proven win–win situation. Following this advice will lead to success, while ignoring it is flirting with failure.

Launch from the Top Down and from the Bottom Up

Starting from the top with an uplifting service initiative makes sense. When high-level leaders speak up and role-model with commitment, it's easier for everyone else to follow—and take the lead at their own levels. This is why Leadership Alignment is first on the Implementation Roadmap and why the Lead section of this book precedes the Build, Learn, and Drive sections.

However, a top-down approach on its own can leave your leaders in an uncomfortable position. Launching from the top down means those at the top make the earliest efforts and then wait for the cascade to see practical results. While this is logical—a cascade does not happen overnight—it can be frustrating for leaders who are accustomed to impact quickly following their actions. In fact, a lack of quick and observable impact can cause some leaders to question whether the outcomes will happen at all.

It takes time to achieve measurable gains in market share, reputation, and financial performance—the ultimate objectives in business. And leaders understand that. But in the meantime, it is vital for high-level leaders to see and hear about early successes on the ground. Don't expect the boss to give endless support and sponsorship without hearing about some practical applications, real stories, and uplifting examples they can believe in and tell others about. These do not need to be big breakthroughs or quantum leaps—leaders know that a little precedes a lot. What they need is evidence of practical action inside the organization, and positive impact on the outside.

Do you remember our earlier discussion about achieving the ultimate objectives in business? It all starts with new ideas and actions, which lead to positive compliments and feedback, which lead to higher satisfaction and loyalty scores, which lead to better market share, reputation, and profits. Stories of frontline effort, excellent recoveries, and customer compliments are leading indicators of the ultimate objectives in business. They are a bracing tonic and necessary fuel for high-level service leaders.

Beware of launching from the bottom up without support from the top—the classic mistake of stand-alone "frontline service training programs." It won't take long before a motivated frontline service provider bumps into a supervisor or manager who does not share the understanding or the passion.

One leading tour operator brought its frontline employees a novel campaign called "Be Service Entrepreneurs." The objective was for staff members to make decisions as if they were the owners. Real entrepreneurs have an appetite for risk and are willing to make mistakes. And so did one enthusiastic frontline service provider. He chartered a plane to move customers along when the company's tour bus broke down. It was a gutsy move his customers loved, but two steps up the corporate ladder, it created an unexpected shock. Most of the company's leaders had never heard of this frontline program and were not pleased with this result. The program was quickly retired as word spread throughout the company that "Be Service Entrepreneurs" was no longer supported.

Launching from the top down and from the bottom up at the same time puts a great deal of responsibility on your people in the middle. In the cascade from the top down, middle managers and supervisors must translate the messages into action, connect company objectives to frontline concerns, and make uplifting language appear practical and useful. In the bottom-up bubbling of new ideas and action steps, the middle plays three culture-building roles: praising team members who do a great job, raising good suggestions for higher-level review, and spotlighting road-blocks that require leadership action for removal. Managers and supervisors need recognition and support from above and below to succeed in these essential roles.

What about launching in the middle and letting the top and the bottom follow later? This may be the weakest approach of all. When leaders are not prepared to lead, and the frontline employees are not prepared for action, then asking middle managers to start the journey alone is a formula for pure frustration.

A top-down cascade brings commitment, alignment, and support. A bottom-up program stimulates new ideas and new actions. An activated middle connects, enables, and empowers. Your successful Implementation Roadmap should start with attention to all three.

Help Your Leaders Lead

Deep inside an enormous software company, a team of passion-ately committed individuals works day and night to improve their customers' and partners' experiences. These committed service heroes know that satisfaction is not enough to retain loyalty and gain market share. They want more than quick recovery when things go wrong; they want to prevent things from going wrong in the first place. They want more than just meeting expectations; they are serious about customer delight. And though the company is sprawling and diverse, these employees believe everyone should step up in service, creating the next great experience together.

Unfortunately, their leaders do not seem to agree. Or perhaps they do not understand. During a workshop, one thundered that he was sick and tired of all the problems and simply yelled at his people to "Fix it!" Another took the stage in front of hundreds, with thousands more watching on video around the world and said, "Customer satisfaction is our number one goal. We must strive to meet expectations." Our service heroes cringed.

Demoralized but still committed, they returned to fighting for a cause these leaders did not promote or defend. One of their leaders told me candidly, "We don't have a business case for improving our service. There is no crisis now we need to fix, and even if we do improve our service, we won't make any more money." This is sweet music to their competition's ears. And then, as if to accentuate the complete lack of alignment at the top, yet another senior leader publicly announced, "We must make all our customers deliriously happy. Anything less is failure."

How can anyone reach the top of a large organization and not understand the value of an uplifting service culture? That's an easy question to answer. Most people who reach high leadership positions are experts in their industry. Often they have strong financial skills and equally strong personalities. But rarely are they experts in building or leading a service culture. That's not what earned them bonuses or brought them up the ladder in the first place.

But a winning service culture must have effective service leaders and uplifting leadership teams. If you are one of the passionate and committed service heroes inside your organization, you may need to help your leaders lead. It may seem odd for managers, supervisors, and frontline staff to tell their leaders what to do—but who else is going to give them help if you won't step up to do it?

You can help your leaders lead by creating opportunities for them to walk the talk, talk the talk, and model uplifting service.

Organizing a customer meeting, focus group, or panel discussion? Invite your leaders to join you, and brief them well when they arrive. Holding a team meeting, cross-functional workshop, or problem-solving session about service issues? Let your leaders know in advance and ask them to stop by to hear the new ideas. Have you got a method for recognition of top-notch service providers? Ask your leaders to participate with a visit, a handshake, a photograph, and a short speech.

Afraid your leaders don't know what to say? Then take the initiative and take responsibility to help your leaders lead. Write short descriptions of service problems that have been recently solved: Who worked on the problem? What did they do? and, How has service been improved? Many of these examples exist inside any organization, but rarely do the details make it to the top.

Concerned your leaders don't see the impact, power, or competitive necessity of uplifting service? Then clip or snip interesting stories about other service leaders—or service disasters—and send them up with a handwritten note sharing your admiration or concern. Or you can organize a benchmarking visit, and invite your leaders to come along. They are too busy to make the visit on the date? Send them a single page report of what you saw, what you learned, and what you will apply.

Afraid customer service is simply lost on the busy agenda of your leaders? Then organize an executive summary of current complaints—and what you are doing about them. Add to this a few carefully selected compliments you have received. Some leaders are drawn to trouble—and your summary will attract their attention. Others are in need of some uplifting themselves, and the compliments you send up the chain of command will be most welcome.

First Choose Your Target,
Then Fire at the Bull's-Eye

One of my clients launched a vigorous service improvement program to create greater value for external customers. Hundreds of classes were conducted for thousands of Service Champions around the world. The business objectives were clear: reclaim market share and rebuild a slipping reputation. Bounce back in recovery situations. Focus on external customer experience, not internal political issues. Demonstrate passion for existing customers. Go all-out to win new business.

But something unusual happened as the program rollout expanded. Rather than focusing on these identified external business targets, earning high internal course evaluations became the course leaders' primary focus. Being rated highly as a very engaging course leader was viewed as great success. Scoring 9 out of 10 for leading a wonderful class became a cause for celebration. That's a great score, but a very different bull's-eye.

Customer success and better business results are why the program was originally conceived. High course leader scores are not the same as valuable business impact. Eventually this lack of alignment became painfully apparent—the focus had drifted away from the early goals, and the entire program needed to refocus. Don't let this drifting happen to you.

A clear bull's-eye should always be at the center of your efforts, well articulated and understood by everyone involved. Your goals can be externally or internally focused. External goals are the improvements you commit to achieve for people outside our organization: customers, clients, partners, distributors, and suppliers. Internal goals are also completely valid targets: improvements in collaboration, performance, engagement, retention, and more. It is fine to have more than one key target, as long as each target is consistent with the others. For example, aiming to reduce complaints and increase sales are naturally aligned targets. Higher levels of employee engagement and excellent course leader scores are very compatible objectives.

My clients often ask how they can measure the Return on Investment (ROI) from a service improvement. They want assurance that their investment will reliably move the needle. I always reply with a simple question: "Tell us specifically what you want to achieve. Which needle measuring results do you want to move?" When I hear a meandering answer lacking clarity and focus, or a wish list of every possible improvement, then I know it is not yet time to start. Don't launch your service improvement efforts until you are crystal clear about your measure of success. Don't pull back the string until you are aiming at the bull's-eye.

One way to increase the odds of impact from your investment is by asking each participant at the end of the program this sequence of five questions.

1. What did you enjoy about this learning experience? This question creates appreciation for the opportunity.
2. What actions will you take to apply what you have learned? This question encourages reflection and review.
3. How will you apply what you have learned? What new actions will you take? Answering this question requires focus, thought, and planning.
4. What value will your actions create for customers or colleagues? The answer to this question should land clearly on your chosen bull's-eye.
5. What is the ROI from your participation and your actions? This question weighs value created against investments in time, cost, and effort.

For some team members, this will be the first time they have been asked to consider the value of their learning and the impact of their actions—which is exactly what you want everyone to think about, appreciate, and improve.

Take the Slow Road to the Fast Track

The principles of uplifting service are so empowering and the practices so effective that some leaders push their teams to solve the most difficult and complex service problems right away. That's a mistake to avoid. Warming up a machine before you go full throttle is good practice. Warming up your service team with a series of "early wins" is good practice, too.

One large company in global logistics applied the methods in this book to improving a series of transactions including customer visits, operational review meetings, and a prospect's experience from inquiry to completed contract. After early success with a fairly easy project, improving customer on-site visits, the regional manager dramatically raised the bar. He asked his team to work on improving the customer's experience when the company responded to complaints. This was one of its most challenging service transactions, with legal and financial implications.

With only a thin layer of past experience and a high threshold of challenge, the service team stalled and struggled. Eventually team members applied the principles of uplifting service and worked their way to success, but the experience was emotionally exhausting. It didn't have to be this way.

When planning a sequence of service problems to tackle, take a gradual approach. Build momentum with early wins on easy issues. Let your team taste the pleasure of uplifting service success. Highlight achievements and celebrate the compliments you earn. Restrain the urge to work on your toughest problems first—their day to be conquered will come.

The same is true when choosing participants for an uplifting service program. Some hard-nosed managers will challenge a new program by sending their most cynical and problematic employees. Their view is, "If a new program can work on these tough nuts, then perhaps it has some merit." But the opposite approach will work much better. What you want in the early days of your journey is good feelings, good results, and good gossip. That comes more easily from participants who want to participate and are eager to succeed.

There is an old saying that "A rising tide lifts all boats." This is also true when building an uplifting service culture—except for those who are stuck in the mud. Practicing generous action raises everyone to a higher level—except those who will not budge. For deeply cynical, resentful, or unwilling employees, there are two successful options. First, they may come to see the light and climb on board for an unfamiliar but uplifting ride. And second, they may feel so out of place as everyone else moves ahead, they no longer feel welcome, and leave. For the success of your organization, either outcome is welcome.

Connect the Building Blocks Together

Visit a building site before construction begins and you will see stacks of lumber, bags of cement, pallets piled high with bricks, cartons of floor tiles, and many doors and windows waiting to be installed. Visit the same site months later and you will see a house, an office, or a building. It's not the building materials that changed, but the way they are connected to each other. It's the connections between the blocks that allows new value to be created: a living room, a conference room, a factory or a store.

Architects understand that connections deliver the value: open spaces encourage open thinking, and closer quarters encourage closer teams. They engineer the outcome from the start by designing for function, beauty, economy and strength.

The 12 Building Blocks of Service Culture offer a similar opportunity for building greater strength. They are useful separately, but their real power comes when you knit them tightly together. Connecting the 12 Building Blocks is like epoxy glue, holding your culture firmly in place and making it stronger than ever.

When guests check out of Marina Bay Sands, they are sent a link by email to a survey seeking feedback about their stay. The first section asks about "Your Overall Experience," and the first question is simply "How was your stay at Marina Bay Sands?" You have four choices: Very Good, Good, Poor, and Very Poor. Of course the integrated resort is aiming for Very Good, but occasionally a guest clicks on the other end of the spectrum. The moment a guest clicks on Very Poor, a white box pops up on the screen with this message: "We do apologize. Please tell us more so we can fix it." Whatever a guest types into this box is carefully studied, and is shared with service teams in the morning "Jump Start" meeting the very next day. The guest is also called or contacted by email with a personal apology and an inquiry about how the resort can set things right.

Let's look at what is happening here from a Building Blocks perspective. The survey accumulates satisfaction scores (Service Measures and Metrics) and, if the customer is unhappy, asks for a written comment (Voice of the Customer). This feedback is studied and sent to the departments that can do something about it (Service Improvement Process), and is shared with all team members in the morning meeting (Service Communications). And Marina Bay Sands contacts the guest directly, seeking an opportunity to bounce back (Service Recovery and Guarantees).

Imagine a contest for service improvement (Service Improvement Process) based on comments received from customers (Voice of the Customer). The contest includes praise and awards for the best improvement ideas (Service Rewards and Recognition). The contest is promoted and winners are applauded on the company website, newsletter, and in quarterly town hall meetings (Service Communications). During final-stage interviews job applicants are asked how they might handle the same situations (Service Recruitment). And new hires study past contest winners as examples of service culture in action during their first few days on the job (Service Orientation).

Learning Your Own Lessons

One nice thing about learning from experience is you often get another chance to try. For example, you may find yourself out of balance from time to time: too much work, too much to eat, not enough exercise, not enough rest, not enough time enjoying life. The good thing is you can always do something about it. As long as you are alive, you get another moment, another chance to do things better. And you can learn from the experience. The same is true in service.

Another upside in learning from experience is you don't have to do everything all at once. For example, if you want to build a healthy body, you can take many actions. You can improve what you eat, drink more water, do some exercise, get more sleep, manage your stress, or clean up the environment around you. You can start with a change in any of these areas and feel the benefits right away. If you work on several of these at once, your benefits will rapidly grow. Your effort to improve will be rewarded. The same is true in service.

CHAPTER 27

More Than a Business Philosophy

Todd Nordstrom shook my hand as the taxi driver loaded his bags into the car. It was 4:30 a.m., pitch black, and the streets of Singapore were silent.

"Do you get it?" I asked him. "Do you understand this whole uplifting service thing?"

"Yes," he responded, vigorously squeezing my hand. "I can't believe more organizations don't understand how powerful this can be. This was an incredible experience."

We continued to shake hands, sharing something important and meaningful in his departing moment.

"Thank you," he said. "I really mean that."

I smiled. "You are most welcome."

Todd climbed into the cab and waved through the window. I watched the taxi's taillights vanish into the darkness en route to Changi Airport, back where this story began.

I assumed Todd would be jet-lagged when he got home. I assumed he would be thinking about what he had seen and learned in Singapore, and that his attention would naturally be focused on service. And I assumed that I would hear back from him within a week—after he had many opportunities in his life to experience true acts of uplifting service, or maybe upsetting service encounters.

On the last assumption, I was wrong. I received this email from Todd before he even left the Los Angeles airport.

To: Ron Kaufman
From: Todd Nordstrom
Subject: I get it now!

Dear Ron,
I get it now. The reason you smile, the reason you're so passionate, and the reason you chase this uplifting service concept is so much bigger than business. I'll talk to you soon.
Respectfully,
Todd

I wondered what he meant. Two days later, I called to ask him.

"When we landed I had to wait forever for my bag," he said. "And the people were rude. Everyone was cranky. I actually heard one lady scold another because she stepped in front of her to grab her suitcase. And then, this guy snapped at the security staff because a dog sniffed the fruit in his bag. It was crazy. And it was exactly what I expected.

"Then I stood in the customs line for almost half an hour," he said. "The room was packed with people and their bags. Everyone was tired. Some of the agents were being unpleasant. I was so frustrated. And I wasn't the only one."

"But?" I asked. "There's got to be something positive, right?"

Todd hesitated.

"Yes," he said. "It was completely unexpected. It was surprising. And, it was really delightful."

He explained that through all of the madness of the airport, he needed to catch a connecting flight to his hometown of Phoenix, Arizona. This meant that after he arrived at one terminal, he had to get his bags and go through customs, and then carry all his bags to another terminal.

"I didn't even know what terminal I was in," he said. "I was groggy from jet lag and exhausted by the long wait for my suitcase to arrive. So I approached the information desk to ask for directions. But after what I had just been through, to tell you the truth I wasn't expecting much help."

Todd approached the information desk asking for directions to the other terminal. He told me how one of the ladies behind the counter responded, saying, "Honey, you've got a long walk ahead of you." But then an older gentleman with white hair at the counter spoke to him, too.

"You look tired," he said. "Come on, I'll walk with you and show you where it is."

"How far is it?" asked Todd.

"I'll show you," said the man. "My name is Richard."

"Ron," Todd said over the phone. "This was not an easy distance—especially for Richard, who seemed to walk with a bit of a limp. But, the guy insisted. And as we walked he asked me questions about my trip, my job, my family, and my kids. That's when I realized something different was happening. I would have been happy with directions, but it made Richard happy to serve."

Todd and I both stopped talking for a moment, agreeing without having to say any words.

Then he spoke with a different tone. A bit deeper and stronger and at the same time more peaceful.

"Uplifting Service is a business philosophy," he said. "I saw that clearly on my trip. But, Richard wasn't walking with me because it was his business. It just meant more to him to do something extra for me."

"You do get it," I said smiling. "You do."

The Proven Path Continues

Months after Todd flew back to his home and family, I visited many of the organizations mentioned in this book: Changi Airport, NTUC Income, Marina Bay Sands, Singapore's government, and others. In every case, these iconic organizations had moved farther along the proven path. For those distinguished by uplifting service this path is never ending. It is an open space for continuous innovation and expression of commitment.

Changi Airport is continuously upgrading its people, technology and terminal buildings to provide more personalized, surprising and stress-free service. The transit areas have been extended for better passenger flow. New floor space has been created for enhanced shopping and dining experiences. Natural light cascades into the terminal building, blending the interior with Singapore's tropical exterior in an eco-friendly combination. New interactive multi-media projects are introduced as technology offers exciting opportunities to connect passengers with resources, business associates and family members around the world.

Changi Experience Agents now patrol the airport proactively seeking visitors and passengers to assist. This special team of multi-lingual customer service officers is deployed at key locations during peak periods where the busy environment can lead to higher levels of stress. Armed with tablet technology and management support, Changi Experience Agents are empowered to assist anyone with special requirements, missing baggage, late flights, tight connections, or any other needs.

At NTUC Income, the cultural revolution from conservative to contemporary has been achieved, and now the company is embarking on another evolution from excellent service to extraordinary. The company has put orange three-wheeler motorcycles on the nation's highways to help drivers by the side of the road, whether they are the company's customers or not. This "Orange Force" started as an initiative to provide safe and reliable assistance for customers in need, but soon became much more. Seventy percent of these roadside engagements do not even call for help. NTUC Income's riders

> "All the mass in the world is an empty channel for the conveyance of your spirit in the realization of their spirit. That's what service really is."
>
> *Junah Boda*

301

discover them on the spot while they patrol the country, looking for opportunities to serve. And 50 percent of those assisted are not even customers of the company, but the "Orange Force" drivers are on the scene and pleased to help.

Marina Bay Sands has solved many of the operational issues that first challenged the world's largest integrated resort. The Journey to Magnificence continues. Ten thousand team members are growing more connected to their careers and to each other. Functional leaders are thinking outside the box to solve unconventional problems and to seize unprecedented opportunities: cross-promotions, sustainable energy, and deeper connections with the world and with the nation.

The country of Singapore continues to mature. Citizen initiatives are growing stronger. The government takes an encouraging position as catalyst for the future, connecting the contributions of many commercial and community groups.

Driving all this progress is more than commercial concerns. It is the underlying purpose to improve the lives of others and ourselves. It is the overarching passion to do so in ways that uplift everyone involved. This commitment to uplifting service is more than a way of doing business, a tactic for winning market share, or simply getting what you want. It is a strategy that cultivates sincere devotion. It is a method with deep meaning built right in.

Uplifting Service is a joyful way of living life together. This proven path brings out the best from ourselves and the best from each other. Uplifting Service is an invitation and a celebration—to give, to live, and to love.

Author's
Acknowledgments

I would like to extend my gratitude to the following individuals for their valuable contributions through interviews, telephone calls, emails, and statements on websites, listed here in order of their appearance in the book and with their titles at the time: Mr. Foo Sek Min, Executive Vice President of Airport Management, Changi Airport Group; Mr. Andrew Hurt, General Manager, Xerox Emirates; Dr. Tan See Leng, CEO and Managing Director, Parkway Health; Mr. Rajeev Suri, CEO, Nokia Siemens Networks; Mr. Melvin Leong, Manager of Corporate and Marketing Communications, Changi Airport Group; Mr. Tan Suee Chieh, CEO, NTUC Income; Mr. Tom Arasi, founding CEO, Marina Bay Sands; Mr. George Tanasijevich, President and CEO, Marina Bay Sands; Mr. Paul Jones, CEO, LUX* Island Resorts; Mr. Tony Hsieh, CEO, Zappos; Mr. Lanham Napier, CEO, Rackspace; Ms. Stephanie Cox, Vice President of Human Resources, Schlumberger; Mr. Jeffrey Becksted, Head of Customer Experience and Service Excellence, Nokia Siemens Networks; Ms. Usha Rangarajan, General Manager Mission Quality, Wipro; Mr. Matthew Daines, Director of Quality and Process Management, Marina Bay Sands; and Mr. Sim Kay Wee, Senior Vice President of Cabin Crew, Singapore Airlines.

My sincere appreciation to Kevin Small, my literary agent, who has uplifted me throughout the book development process, to Karen Kreiger at Evolve Publishing for being a truly delightful partner in bringing this message to the world, and to the team at Bookmasters for their efficiency and expertise. Thanks to Todd Nordstrom and his keen ear for capturing and creating uplifting stories, to Keri Childers, my book marketing director, for her passionate belief in our message, and to Bill Chiaravalle, for his elegant visualization of this book's cover and interior design.

I am thankful every day for the worldwide team at UP! Your Service who enable our contribution to others with their commitment to uplifting service, including Steven Howard, Richard Farrell, Darren Sim, Aristotle Motii Nandy, Naile McLoughlin, Tania Sng, Daryl See, Shawn Chua, Adrian Ho, Anne Tay, Sherman Cheow, Chee Seow Hui, Wong Lai Chun, Lynn Chea, Jane Foo, Carmen Chang, Cyril Tjahja, Apple Chua, Tay Chee Wei, Joanne Esta Chong, Janet Tan, Bruce Keats, Sharon Teo, Foo Teck Leong, Jason Tan, Noelita Superio, Carole Harris, Franco Arollado, Charles Tang, Mitchel Quek, Shyam Kumar, Jeff Eilertsen, Andrea Ihara, Jacqueline Chia, Betsy Dickinson, and Dan Haygeman, and our deeply appreciated advisors and partners through the years, including Junah Sowojay Boda, Dean Barrett Hazeltine, Professor Jochen Wirtz, Chiew Yu Sarn, Audrey Yap, Roger Hamilton, Philip Hallstein, David Hall, Omar Khan, Richard, Veronica and Grace Tan, Ram, Gautam, Panna and Jay Ganglani, Gopal Chandnani, Vijay Tirathrai, Dinesh Senan, John Ong, Winston Chan, Su-Anne Chia, Philippa Huckle, Richard Wilson, Jonathan Bonsey, Øistein Kristiansen, Zandra Marie, Nolan Tan, Lim Suu Kuan, Delphine Ang, Mike and Monette Hamlin, Yazan Hatamleh, Navaid Khan, Todd Lapidus, Richard Whiteley, Pat Smith, Valerie and Russell Bishop, Saqib Rasool, Tim Munson, Luke Wyckoff, Rick Curzon, Ray Jefferson, Robin

Speculand, Les McKeown, Shiv Kumar, Mrigank Ohja, Perry Fagan, Rameshwari Ramachandra, Poorani Thanusha and Landmark Education, Helen Lim and Capelle Academy, Sally Chew and Temasek Polytechnic, Scott Coady and Sage Alliance Partners, Leslie Lim and Pansing Distributors, the Adam Khoo Learning Technologies Group, Biz-Era.net, Rainbow Print, Tien Wah Press, C2Workshop, Verztec, and Krawler Technologies.

I have tremendous admiration for the hundreds of Client Leaders, Program Leaders, and Certified Course Leaders who have brought UP! Your Service College courses to thousands of Uplifting Service Champions in an extraordinary range of companies, countries, government agencies, and cultures throughout the world. You are too numerous to list here by name, yet each one of you holds a special place in my heart, as your efforts make it possible for customers and colleagues to be served, and cultures to become transformed.

My lifelong appreciation to Fernando Flores, Chauncey Bell and Christopher Davis for their teaching and coaching in ontological design which so profoundly shapes my view of the world and passion for designing it with others.

Heartfelt thanks to my grandparents, my parents and my wife's parents who have been generous role models of service all their lives, and to my daughter, Brighten Kaufman, who shares my creative love for life and passion for uplifting other people.

With grace I extend my hand in admiration and appreciation to Jenny Kaufman, my infinitely supportive wife, business partner, best friend and scuba diving buddy, for her acceptance, encouragement and contributions every day. Without her, this book would not be in your hands.

And finally to you, the reader of this book, I extend my heartfelt admiration and respect. May your life be uplifted as you uplift the lives of others.

This world is a better place because of YOU.

Index

Tools *for*
Your Journey

Every great expedition begins with a great idea. However, embarking on your journey into a new world also requires planning, commitment, and the right set of tools. Great explorers prepare themselves with proper gear and resources. To help you succeed along the path, we have provided all the tools you will need to uplift your service performance and build an uplifting service culture—free articles, videos, and easy to follow guides—revealing new ways you can begin transforming your culture today.

Get these FREE resources
now at UpliftingService.com

Article Library
Hundreds of tips, techniques, and real best practice examples with action steps you can apply right away. Learn what you can do right now to improve your service performance and build a stronger service culture.

Video Library
Innovative ideas and useful insights. Watch these short videos to understand the benefits, issues, and challenges in building an uplifting service culture. You will learn a lot in just a few short minutes.

Assessments
Are you an Uplifting Service Provider? Take the quiz to find out. Are you an Uplifting Service Leader? Take the test to discover your rating. Do you have an Uplifting Service Culture? Find out now.

Webinars
Ron Kaufman explains how the Uplifting Service architecture works, and how you can put it to work right away. Each webinar is packed with case study examples, insights, and results. You can learn more online, anytime, at your convenience.

Posters, Screen Savers, and Slide Shows
Beautiful images and inspiring quotations to uplift everyone where you work and live. Colorful posters are in high-resolution format for you to print, hang on your walls, and enjoy. Slide shows can be used for meetings and special events. Attractive screen savers to uplift you when you are serving others.

Quotations on Service
Thousands of quotations on service from the author, Ron Kaufman, and other famous people. Enjoy and share these meaningful words of wisdom.

Get these
FREE
resources now at
UpliftingService.com

Join *the* Uplifting Service Community

Join Ron Kaufman and many thousands of Uplifting Service enthusiasts, sharing the latest news, ideas, discussions, inspiration, and advice. Get answers to your questions, and advice from around the world to solve your service problems. Community members are committed to upgrading service performance, building strong service cultures, and uplifting the spirit of service providers worldwide.

Email Newsletter ⋯▸ **UpYourService.com/subscribe**

Subscribing to INSIGHTS is the best way of keeping in touch with UP! Your Service and Ron Kaufman. You will receive free articles, videos, white papers, and other valuable tools for improving service performance and building an Uplifting Service culture.

UP! Your Service Blog ⋯▸ **UpYourService.com/blog**

The UP! Your Service blog is an open community for committed service leaders, managers, and providers. We are dedicated to creating a world where people are educated and inspired to excel in service to others. We welcome your views and participation.

Ron Kaufman Video Blog ⋯▸ **RonKaufman.com/blog**

Follow Ron Kaufman on his service adventures around the world. If you want to know where the world's leader in Uplifting Service is and who he is serving, this is the blog to watch.

LinkedIn ⋯▸ **LinkedIn.com/in/ronkaufman**

If you are a senior leader or manager responsible for the service culture in your organization, you can connect with Ron Kaufman through the world's largest professional networking community.

Facebook ⋯▸ **Facebook.com/RonKaufmanUPYourService**

Be a fan of Ron Kaufman and Uplifting Service on Facebook. Like this page to enjoy all the latest news, photographs, and updates. Follow Ron Kaufman around the world.

Twitter ⋯▸ **@RonKaufman/ @UpYourService**

Follow on Twitter for instant updates on what's happening, including tips, insights, and ideas from everywhere in the world of Uplifting Service.

YouTube ⋯▸ **YouTube.com/RonKaufman**

The online video home where you can enjoy hundreds of videos by Ron Kaufman and others in the Uplifting Service community. This is where one of the world's top-rated speakers turns it ON for your education and enjoyment.

About
UP! Your Service

UP! Your Service enables leaders and organizations

to dramatically upgrade service performance, and secure a sustainable advantage by building an uplifting service culture.

If you are a CEO or leader of a large organization looking to improve your service or to differentiate on service, UP! Your Service delivers proven solutions quickly and economically.

The UP! Your Service methodology aligns and accelerates activity in the five areas outlined in *Uplifting Service*: WHY, LEAD, BUILD, LEARN, and DRIVE. This integrated top-down and bottom-up approach leads to an action-oriented culture empowering everyone to delight customers and colleagues with consistently uplifting service.

UP! Your Service educational courses and programs build uplifting skill sets and mindsets, scaling quickly and effectively with in-house resources. These programs have been proven effective in diverse industries, cultures, and countries worldwide, including translation into fourteen languages.

With offices in Singapore and North America, UP! Your Service works with businesses, associations, and government agencies throughout the world.

EMAIL / WEB:

Enquiry@UpYourService.com

UpYourService.com

Meet
Ron Kaufman

Ron Kaufman is the world's

premiere thought-leader, educator, and motivator for uplifting customer service and building service cultures. Ron is a regular columnist at *Bloomberg Businessweek* and the author of 14 other books on service, business, and inspiration.

Ron provides powerful insights from working with clients all over the world in every major industry for more than twenty years. Ron is an inspiration to leaders and managers with his content rich and entertaining speeches, and his impactful, interactive workshops. He is rated one of the world's "Top 25 Who's Hot" speakers by *Speaker Magazine*.

Ron has been featured in *The Wall Street Journal*, *The New York Times*, and *USA Today*. He is passionately committed to uplifting the spirit and practice of service worldwide.

EMAIL / WEB:

Enquiry@RonKaufman.com

RonKaufman.com